I0166914

A Salary Cinderella Story

(Or How To Make More Money Without A Fairy Godmother)

Laura C. Browne and Jill L. Ferguson

In Your Face Ink LLC

First published 2019
by In Your Face Ink LLC
9524 Camelback Road, #130-182
Glendale, AZ 85305
© 2019 In Your Face Ink LLC

The right of Laura C. Browne and Jill L. Ferguson to be identified as authors of this work has been asserted by them in accordance with sections 77 and 78 of the Copyright, Designs and Patent Act of 1988.

All rights reserved. No part of this book may be reprinted or reproduced or utilized in any form or by any electronic, mechanical or other means, now known or hereafter invented, including photocopying and recording, or in any information storage or retrieval system, without permission in writing from the publishers.

Trademark notice: Product or corporate names may be trademarks or registered trademarks, and are used only for identification and explanation without intent to infringe.

Names: Browne, Laura C. and Ferguson, Jill L., authors Title: A Salary Cinderella Story (Or How to Make More Money Without a Fairy Godmother/Laura C. Browne and Jill L. Ferguson.

Identifiers: ISBN 9780692041536 (pbk)

Subjects: Vocational guidance | Women in Business

To working women everywhere who want more recognition and money, this book is for you.

Chapter 1

The airport was exceptionally busy even for a Monday, thought El Casey, as she scanned the crowd in the food court looking for an empty seat. She balanced the orange plastic tray of hot tea and chicken chow mein in one hand while wrestling her suitcase behind her. It was supposed to be a roller board, but just that morning one of the wheels decided to lock up intermittently so that it no longer rolled.

Her boyfriend called this prime *touron* time (his word for what he dubbed "tourist-morons" or those who travelled infrequently and so were uneducated about how to quickly go through security with all of its ever-evolving regulations). Security had taken extra long, even though El had TSA Pre-Check.

El was sure that the stubborn suitcase, and all of the challenges leading up to this business trip were a sign of even worse things to come. Her boss had insisted she fly to Florida to placate a client who never seemed to be satisfied, and El was convinced that like Mick Jagger, they would be forever singing that same refrain.

A family with two squirmy kids offered her their table as they rose to leave. "Thank you," El said as she pulled out a chair. El was grateful for the space, despite the ketchup smears and stickiness. She splashed a bit of water from her bottle and scrubbed the tabletop with a napkin. Getting gunk on her grey suit was not an option. Her clothes may have been bought second hand and from clearance racks, but she was fastidious in the garments' care. She didn't buy into Granny's idea of cleanliness equating godliness, but El did think it equaled professionalism and appeased her compulsion for neatness.

Her phone beeped alerting that it was 20 minutes until boarding, so she dug into the chow mein, careful not to drip any soy sauce as she slurped the noodles. She eyed the fortune cookie in its plastic wrapper. She loved that the Chinese awarded words of wisdom in tasty, vaguely vanilla cookies to eaters of their cuisine.

When she could wait no longer, she burst the cellophane and cracked the cookie. *You have a good head for matters of money.* El laughed aloud. "Dumbest fortune cookie ever. I have no head for money," she said to the cookie. But Derek, she thought, is like that Snoop Dogg song *with his mind on money*…and on little else. When she first met Derek's parents, they joked that it must have been her green, green eyes that attracted their son. He had been obsessed with money and all things green since he negotiated his first "salary", as he called it, at age five for feeding the family dog.

Now he handled mergers and acquisitions for a company he partially owned, while launching a part-time venture capital start-up on the side, while she was paid way less than she thought she was worth, and creatively tried to juggle student loans, car payment, rent, food for her and the cat who had adopted her, and a bit of credit card debt. All these things felt less like balls in the air than pin-pulled hand grenades. She sighed, stood, and shoved the stupid slip of paper into her pocket. El checked the security of the clip holding back her shoulder length auburn hair. She straightened her skirt, emptied the tray into a nearby garbage can, and marched off towards the gate. Her suitcase bumped behind her like an obstinate toddler.

Once on the plane in her window seat, client file on her lap for one last review during the flight, El watched the neighboring planes being readied for take-off. She dreamed of flying to Tahiti or Fiji or somewhere more exotic than Florida and relaxing on the beach with a potent and sweet rainbow colored, fruity drink. But her vacation dreams were interrupted by a loud, "Excuse me. Excuse me. Woman with a cane coming through."

El looked up and was stunned at the woman's high cheek bones, black unruly curls, and obviously expensive outfit. Cane woman wore a fitted fuchsia suit, black belt at its waist, and a bright white dress shirt. Her one foot was enclosed in a black medical boot and the other sported a black sneaker, and she hobbled with the help of black cane with a carved cherry wooden handle. "Takes forever to go seven rows," she said to El when she stopped. "It's not that difficult, people. Stop. Put bag overhead and sit down." And she did just that, sitting in the aisle seat in El's row. El smiled at the woman.

"PJ. That's P period J period. My parents named me Patience as kind of joke, I think. I came into the world weeks early and have had no patience for anything ever since, including how long my name is, so I go by my initials." She extended her hand.

El extended her own. "El. It's nice to meet you," though El thought that might not be true.

"And El is short for Ellen? Eloise? Eleanor? Elaine?" PJ clicked her seatbelt closed.

"El is short for Ella. Cinderella, actually, so maybe your parents weren't the only ones with a sense of humor."

"Wow. I can only imagine the evil stepsister jokes—"

"Or how many times I've heard bibbidi-bobbidi-boo," El cut in. "But the truth is, my mom is from near Philly and never got over a guy from high school. A guy who started the band Cinderella—"

"No!" PJ cut in. "The glam band?"

"Yep. So I'll take bibbidi-bobbidi-boo over Nobody's Fool any day."

"Wow. Now Patience doesn't seem as big of a burden." She waved a ring hand to flag the passing flight attendant. "Dear, when we get airborne, my new friend and I need a drink."

After they had settled in, PJ asked El why she was traveling.

El looked down and sighed. "My boss is sending me. I have to visit a client. They're unhappy and the salesperson wants me to go along to the meeting."

"What's wrong with that?" asked PJ, sipping her white wine.

"Well, I guess nothing really. It's just that..." El paused for a minute, not sure how much she should share. She took a sip of her own white wine. "I'm just frustrated. I work like crazy and it wouldn't bother me so much, but my boss doesn't even seem to notice. I mean he notices when there's a problem but...not the rest of the time." She shrugged.

"I see. And...?" prompted PJ.

"And some days I just wonder if it's worth it. I mean, I like what I do, but maybe I'm in the wrong place." It was the first time El voiced this aloud, and she was a bit taken aback that it came out of her mouth to a stranger.

"Why do you think that? What do you think is going on?"

El found the answers to PJ's questions coming easily so she took another sip of the wine and continued. "Well, there's Carl. He just got promoted and I haven't been promoted in more than two years."

There was a slight smile on PJ's face as she asked, "Why do you think he was promoted?"

"That's just it, I don't know. I work harder and spend more time on projects that he does. He seems to spend time brown-nosing and chatting with co-workers instead of getting things done." The pitch of her voice rose as her frustration vented.

El complained a few more minutes. Suddenly she felt uncomfortable that she had been hogging the conversation so she said, "Enough about me. Why are you flying today?"

PJ leaned back in her seat and smiled. "I'm going to speak at a conference."

"What kind of a conference?"

"A conference for women in my industry."

El was intrigued but also a little embarrassed about all the complaining she had done. "Really? What's your topic?"

PJ smiled and said, "My message is how they can make more money at work by changing just one thing."

El stared at her and thought about the fortune cookie. "Okay, I'm all ears. What's the one thing?"

PJ leaned forward, paused for effect, and looked around as though she was checking to see if anyone in the other rows was listening. "You have to ask."

El started to laugh and stopped herself. "What do you mean?"

"Just what I said: if you want to make more money at work, you have to ask for it."

El shook her head. "That's it. I just have to ask? And they'll give me more money?"

"Of course, there is a little more to it than that but that's the main idea."

El shook her head again. "That's way too simple. It's like Yoda saying, 'Do. Or do not. There is no try.'"

PJ chuckled. "It is a simple concept, but you'd be surprised how often we don't ask for what we really want. We women try by hoping and hinting for what we want, but we really don't come out and ask for it. That is the do. People won't read our minds and give us things. We make it easier for others to understand us by stating what we want."

El paused and thought for a moment, as PJ continued. "For example, in your situation, you want a promotion, right? Have you directly asked your boss for a promotion?"

"Well, no but…"

PJ interrupted her, waving her bejeweled fingers around. "Exactly, that's what I mean. How can you expect your boss to know you want a promotion?"

El stammered, "I…I…I mean, I mean, it's obvious. Everyone wants a promotion. He should know."

PJ grinned. "He should know," she repeated. "El, nobody else can read your mind. Not even Yoda. Many women complain that their significant others don't do this or that. They think their partners should know what they want. Trust me, it doesn't work at home and it doesn't work at work."

El stared at the seatback in front of her and thought about Derek. While she tried to anticipate his needs and gauge his moods, she often felt that he didn't understand her. He called the cat "a mooch" and "a drain on resources she didn't have." When she told him about her student loans or how her rent had gone up ten percent this year, she thought maybe he'd give her financial advice. But all he said was, "I can't believe you'd pay so much for this dump," and went back to watching the Golden State Warriors win another championship on her television.

She turned back to PJ, who had finished her wine and seemed to be waiting. "I can see your point," El said, and then drained her own plastic cup, balled the napkin, and placed it inside the cup. Her best friends Leticia and Teresa also complained about their bosses and the promotions they didn't get. Almost every week they met for happy hour and commiserated about adult life after college, their jobs, their dating lives, and their lack of progress towards life goals. They were nearing thirty and had expected to be so much farther along by now. Could it really be that easy? Could they have more from life, if only they asked for it?

"But...?" PJ prompted.

"But it sounds a bit like new age abundance B.S., if you forgive me for saying so."

PJ laughed. "I'm not talking about some kind of name it and claim it philosophy. My point is that women, in particular, in the work place, don't speak up for ourselves or tell our leaders what we want. We expect rewards for our diligence, for our long hours, for our hard work, but we don't want to toot our own horns. Think about the brown-nosing colleague of yours, the one that got the promotion. Why'd you call him a brown-noser?"

"Because he is," El said.

"How?"

El looked puzzled. "Because he is. My friend Leticia uses the phrase 'so far up his boss's butt he can see her stomach'. That describes Carl."

"What does he do that makes you think that?"

"Oh, he brags all of the time about his accomplishments. He sends mass e-mails to the group with updates. And if the boss needs someone to take an action during a meeting, Carl volunteers and makes sure everyone sees him do it, especially if it's a high-profile project where he'll get to interact with the execs. He's like pick me, pick me!" El shook her head in disgust.

PJ smiled. "You know that old squeaky wheel saying, right? Well you can bet that any time Carl has the boss' ear, he's plugging for what he wants. I knew a woman who was super pissed off when she was passed over for an international assignment she really, really wanted. I asked her if she ever told her boss that she wanted that assignment. She told me that her boss should have known. She had been taking Spanish classes for years in case an assignment opened up and her boss knew that. But when she confronted the boss after talking to me, she learned that the boss had no idea she wanted the assignment. She thought she was taking the classes for her own enrichment. The guy who got the job told the boss over and over that if an international assignment ever came up, he wanted it. He even sent her short e-mails or messages every time one came out in another division as a reminder that if a job opened in their division that she should send him. So guess who was first on the boss's mind when the job opened up and who got the job?"

"The guy," El mumbled. She didn't like it. She couldn't see herself acting like "Pick me! Pick me Carl." She was sure he annoyed their whole team. El's stomach felt hollow though when she admitted that may have been what had gotten Carl the promotion. She hated talking about her accomplishments; her mom raised her that it wasn't right to boast.

"Exactly. He got it because he asked."

El sighed and mumbled a bit of scripture she remembered from Sunday school, "I have not because I've asked not."

PJ grinned. "Old wisdom. New Testament book of James. Still applicable to today." She bent down and rummaged in her designer bag, from an emerald green leather card case she pulled a card and handed it to El. "In addition to speaking at conferences, I help women get what they need."

El looked at the card. It was ecru linen with maroon raised letters in two stacked lines:

Patience "P.J." James
Empowerer of Women

followed by a phone number and an e-mail address.

El thought about how miserable she was at work. It would be great to get some advice so she could figure out what to do. "How do you empower women?"

PJ smiled. "I meet with them to discuss their situations and help them to see what they need to do to be more successful. And success doesn't always mean more money. Though who doesn't want more money? Sometimes it means more work/life balance. And sometimes it means finding a job or career that you're really passionate about."

El's mind buzzed with questions, as PJ continued, "I have a day job. This is what I do for fun. My passion, if you will. I like helping other women and I seem to have a knack for it." She smiled. "At least that's what they tell me."

PJ told her how she worked with women to find out what they really want at work and then plan how to get it. She shared several stories about women who were stuck and how they made changes that made big differences.

PJ made it all sound so easy. El looked at her more critically. They were about the same age. How in the hell did she learn this?

PJ explained, "A few years out of college, several of my friends went back to school for their Master's Degrees to get ahead. I looked at my bank account and realized that wasn't for me, so I decided that I was going to get my own Master's Degree, the PJ degree. So I read a ton of books and articles, listened to podcasts from smart people, any way I could learn from others. I also started asking people about their stories. I interviewed women and men to find out what made them successful. What helped them when they had setbacks? What made them keep going? What did they wish they had known about work earlier?

"I used the information in my career and it worked. I had more fun, got more opportunities, and made more money. I started sharing what I had learned with others. It started working for them, too. And that's why I'm here," she finished, "to speak at this conference and to help other women get what they want at work."

"What's the main advice that you give?" asked El.

"That depends on what the issue is," PJ said. "For example, at this conference, I'm talking about how to make more money at work. There are plenty of things that can change that, but the main action women can take is simply to ask for more money. One of my favorite phrases is if you don't ask, you don't get."

More fun? More opportunities? And more money? El longed for more of all three. "That sounds like it would be great. It would be really helpful to me."

PJ nodded and looked into El's green eyes. "Yes, it could be helpful." She paused, as though she was waiting.

The pilot announced for the flight attendants to prepare the cabin for landing. And PJ broke eye contact to put up and secure her tray table.

El did the same, while saying, "It would be so terrific if I could find out about that. I'd really like it if I could get that information."

PJ's eyes were back on El's and PJ grinned. "Yes, it would be nice if people would give you that information. If they would wave a magic wand and it would just appear."

El took a deep breath and decided to say something she normally wouldn't say. After all, what did she have to lose? She didn't know PJ at all. After the flight, she would probably never see her again. "Would you tell me what I can do to get what I want at work?"

PJ laughed. "Yes. And you just learned your first lesson. You need to ask for what you want. Hinting that you want some information and hoping, won't get it for you. Since you've asked, I'll be happy to help you, but I do have two requirements for me to help you."

El braced herself and thought of her tiny bank account. She worried that the grail was before her and she couldn't afford it.

PJ said, "My first requirement is that you have to take action. But action doesn't have to be something I tell you to do; it can be anything that you decide, as long as you move forward with something. I'll be happy to meet with you and give you information, but only if you do something with it. If you're just going to take notes, then I will suggest some great books for you to read because you don't need me.

"My second requirement is that you have to share the information I give you. Some women think that if they share information with others it means less for them. They see work as a pie and if I give you information, there is less of the pie for me. Instead, I say, let's have a bigger pie. When one woman wins, we all win."

"That's all?" El's eyes were wide. "That all sounds great but how much do you charge?"

PJ laughed. "El, I'm not going to charge you anything. This is my opportunity to pay it forward to thank the people who gave me the information when I was getting my PJ Master's Degree."

El couldn't believe it and couldn't say YES fast enough. In the few moments that were left, PJ reviewed the notes for her speech and El looked at the client's folder. They agreed to a video conference the following week.

Chapter 2

The following Monday night El sat in front of her computer and nervously picked at a loose thread at the hem of her navy skirt. *I'm fine. I can do this. It's no big deal*, she said to herself. But it did feel like a big deal. In five minutes she was going to have her first video meeting with PJ. She was torn between excitement and panic. *What if she decides that she doesn't want to help me? Or she decides that I can't do it or I'm not worth her time?* She took a deep breath. *Stop, it's just a conversation. She's a nice person and I'll get some new ideas.*

It didn't help that she had just had a text conversation with Derek and he had been telling her what monthly charges she had to get rid of. The gym membership was stupid since she rarely went and needed to be canceled. Lunch with her co-workers was too expensive, so she'd need to start bringing lunch. She knew he was trying to help her lessen her stress about finances, but sometimes he was bossy and annoying.

She took another deep breath and let it out, trying to blow away the anxiety and tightness she felt in her chest. She concentrated on her notes, which were questions and ideas to cover in the meeting. She wasn't sure what to expect and she wanted to be ready. She put a smile on her face and logged in a few minutes early.

"Hi there, El. How are you doing?" PJ wore a turquoise blue sweater and looked much more relaxed than when they had parted at airport luggage carousel.

"Great, PJ, thanks. How are you? How was the conference?"

"Wonderful. A terrific group of women. I always feel energized when I meet with great people like that." PJ told her a little about the conference and other speakers and then asked, "How was your customer meeting?"

El grimaced. "It wasn't bad. It was just aggravating. We spent two days trying to make the customer happy, and when I got back, I found that they announced a few more promotions. And of course, I wasn't on the list. Not that I expected to be. But it's frustrating to work so hard and see others get rewarded."

"Hmm," said PJ. "Why do you think you're not on the promotion list?"

El launched into her favorite complaints about her boss and company, things she said almost weekly to her best friends and to Derek. PJ stayed silent as El complained about the economy and the unfairness of business culture. When she launched into a diatribe about male bosses and men in general, PJ stopped her by literally holding up her hand like a police officer stopping traffic.

"El, let's change the point of view here. Let's not talk about what other people have done or not done. We can't change anyone else or be certain why they did or didn't do something. Let's talk about you. What did you do to get on the promotion list?"

El didn't know what to say. Her friends normally let her finish her rant. She quickly recovered. "My work. I work really hard and my work should speak for itself."

"And?" PJ's eyebrows were raised.

"What do you mean? I work hard. That should be enough." She considered their conversation on the plane. "And I don't want to be a Carl. I don't want to brown-nose."

PJ laughed. "I agree. The only brown on your nose should be your freckles. Nobody's saying that you need to be Carl or even act like Carl. But it does sound like you could learn a little from Carl. The point is that it's easy to blame and complain about others. It's hard to take a look at what needs to change and take action. How are you holding yourself back? You can't change those other people, but you can change what you do."

El frowned and defended herself. "I do take action. It's not like I sit around and wait for the world to just hand me a promotion. I work my butt off for my company." She hated how the pitch of her voice rose on that last sentence.

"I'm sure you do," PJ said, her voice very even and calm, "but you're not getting what you want. Are you willing to take different actions—not just work hard—to get a different result?"

"But I don't know what else to do." El felt tears of frustration form but she refused to cry.

PJ leaned closer to the camera and quietly said, "That's why we're talking, El. When I was starting out in my career, I got frustrated that I wasn't making enough money or getting interesting opportunities. Somebody told me that Einstein said, 'Insanity is doing the same thing over and over again and expecting different results.' I don't know if he actually said it or not, but it stuck with me and I decided I was going to start taking different actions until I found some that got me the right results."

El stared down at her computer keyboard. She could think of nothing else she could do besides work hard. PJ startled her by asking, "Did you have a hamster when you were a kid?"

El looked up. "Huh?"

"A hamster. Did you have one?"

"My brother did," El said. "He named it Gizmo. It was some kind of long-haired fancy hamster, all gray with a pink little nose and beady black eyes."

"Well think of Gizmo. He probably ran his little hamster legs on a wheel most of the night, right, since hamsters are nocturnal."

"Yeah, he loved that wheel and it drove us crazy. We had to move him from my brother's room to the basement because the wheel squeaked so much." El smiled.

"Right. Classic hamster story. Well, Gizmo ran and ran and ran night after night after night, right? He worked so hard at running. But guess what? Gizmo never got anywhere. And probably the only satisfaction he ever got was the joy of the journey or the run itself...but we'll never know. People, on the other hand, are different, they need to get places. When we work hard, we expect it to get us somewhere."

"Yeah, the only time Gizmo got anywhere was when he escaped the cage. But even then he only crawled into the kitchen cabinets and built himself a shredded paper towel nest." El's eyes sparkled with the memory.

"Exactly," PJ said. "Hamsters are predictable. They are happy doing the same damn thing over and over and over and getting the same results. You're not a hamster, El. It's time to get off the wheel. Take charge of your career. Let's figure out a way to do things differently."

El finally got it and felt inspired. "On the plane you said there was one simple idea that would make a difference—something about asking. Can you tell me about that?"

"Yes, I said that asking for what you want is the key. That's because most women won't ask directly for what they want. There are a few things that support the asking. First, you have to prepare. You have to know your stuff, and be ready to explain why. Then you have to ask in a way that people can really hear and will want to give you what you want."

El was skeptical. "People will want to give me what I want?"

PJ nodded. "That's why preparation is so important. You need to really understand the situation and the people you're working with so you can help them to see that what you want can help them."

"But what if it doesn't?"

PJ laughed. "Well, if it really doesn't help them at all, then you're not going to get what you want. But if you can figure out how you can both benefit and get them to buy in, then they'll help you. Many people though get stressed and just focus on what they want, not on the other person."

El thought about her boss, Tom. She hadn't really thought about what he wanted. She was so focused on why she deserved the promotion.

PJ continued, "And the final part is knowing how to respond. Whether the other person says yes or no, there are some right things to do and some wrong things."

"What do you mean? If the person says no, the answer is no. Why does my response matter?"

"Even if the answer is no, if you handle it right, the answer might change or it could set you up for a yes in the future. And if you say the wrong things when the answer is yes, the other person might wonder if they made a mistake."

El had never thought about that before and wondered how she had reacted when other people said yes. She knew she probably didn't react too well when the answer was no.

PJ continued, "Let's talk about your situation. It sounds like you want a promotion, right? What's important to you about this promotion? Why do you want it?"

"Well, what I really want is to make more money. I want a raise."

"Okay, so let's talk about how to prepare to get that raise."

El smiled and thought I've got this. "I've already gone online and checked out what other people are getting paid." She told PJ about the research she had done.

PJ said, "That's great. But let's back up a bit and talk about how you need to prepare yourself first. I like to say to myself, 'It's only business, it's not personal' and that helps me to remember to keep the emotion out of it when I talk about it."

"But it *is* personal," El said. "We're talking about my job, my raise, my money." Her vocal pitch went up at the end of the sentence, even though she hated when it did that. She thought about what she could do with the extra money. She could splurge by shopping at Trader Joe's instead of the big box super center's grocery store. And she wouldn't have to worry so much about paying the monthly bills and about how much electricity she used. She could finally feel like she was getting ahead. Yeah, it was personal.

"El, I know it's personal to you. Of course it is. The problem is that when we show emotions over something like that instead of treating it like a business project, it can make it more difficult for us to get what we want." PJ paused.

El said, "You mean, when I think about how frustrated I am, it gets in the way?"

"Exactly. Kind of like how the hamster wheel noise got in the way of you and your brother seeing how great the hamster was. Emotions can be internal noise or even external noise that drown out the beauty of what we want and offer. How do you think your manager responds to your emotions?"

El laughed. "Like I'm a squeaky hamster. Tom doesn't react really well when I'm upset about work projects. He's probably not going to want to hear how upset I am about being passed over for promotion. But it's not fair…"

"Nobody ever said life is fair," said PJ and paused.

El considered, blankly staring down at her keyboard again. "I never thought about it this way. On one hand, it doesn't seem fair that I can't show how upset I am about this because it is really important to me… But I guess he doesn't really need to know. On the other hand, I am afraid that if I show how upset I am, it's going to get me even more upset and that would be a problem." She sighed. "Maybe treating it like a problem with a business project could work but I'm not sure, since I admitted I get a bit emotional sometimes about those. I'll have to think about this some more."

PJ nodded. "Of course, you have to do what works for you. In my experience though, managers are more likely to pay attention when the request is well thought out and unemotional. We can talk some more about how to do that."

El looked up from the keyboard and at PJ. "Okay."

"I have another question for you, El. How confident do you feel that you deserve this raise?"

"I already told you I should get it and the research shows I'm underpaid."

"Yes, but how *confident* are you that you should get a raise? Can you comfortably talk to your boss about your raise request?"

"Well that's a different story," said El. "If I was a confident about asking Tom, I probably wouldn't be talking to you now."

PJ smiled. "We can work on preparing you for that. Tell me what worries you the most about asking for a raise."

El said that asking for a raise reminded her of asking her parents if she could go to a concert in another city when she was a teenager. She felt like she had to think up all of the arguments for the "no" answers ahead of time to try to do an end-run around the denial. It was nerve-wracking and exhausting. Why couldn't they reward her good grades, good behavior, and hard work by granting her that one thing?

"Like a fairy godmother?" PJ joked.

El laughed, having been caught off guard. "Exactly. After all, I'm Cinderella." She shrugged and grinned.

"You are Cinderella, but your boss is neither a fairy godmother nor your evil stepmother. And I doubt your parents were either. I think many women are a bit more like Ariel, from the *Little Mermaid*, only they haven't realized that they've lost their voice. Nevertheless, they still need to get it back. And that's what I'm here to help you do: determine how to talk to your boss and be confident so you can get what you want."

"Okay, that sounds great. How do I that?"

"Let me ask you, what's stopping you from feeling confident about asking for a raise?"

"Well, I know I deserve a raise, I mean I think I should get a raise." El paused. "I guess I'm nervous about what my boss is going to say. I don't want to mess things up. I don't want him to be mad at me for asking for a raise."

"Why would he be mad at you?"

"I don't know. He might think I don't appreciate him or what he's done for me…" She trailed off. She thought about her boss. She really did like working for him. He gave her opportunities to do new things and supported her interest in learning different areas. She didn't want to mess things up. She liked her job. Maybe what she had at work was enough. Maybe Derek was right, she should get rid of some expenses and she wouldn't have to go through this.

"And so?" asked PJ. "Do you really think he'd be mad at you?"

"The whole thing is just so uncomfortable," whined El.

PJ smiled. "He should just give you the raise, right?"

El smiled back and nodded. "That would make things a whole lot easier."

"El, let me tell you something. I've talked to plenty of people about what it takes to get a raise and promotion at work and do you know, not one man I've talked to has ever told me that he was worried about upsetting his manager."

"Really?" asked El.

"Really. It's only women who worry about upsetting their bosses. The men I've worked with realize that it's not personal. They don't worry about damaging the relationship with their boss because they expect their boss will just see it as part of the job. And actually, they understand that if they handle the conversation well, their boss will see them as even more valuable because they're good negotiators."

El didn't know what to say. It wasn't the first time that she wondered what went on in men's brains. "So men think that asking for a raise can

20

help the relationship with their bosses?" she asked slowly.

"If it's done right, yes." PJ nodded her head. "I know, it may seem strange, but it's true. Think about it. If you're able to get rid of the emotion and deal with a tricky situation in a professional manner, your boss could be impressed and see that you could handle other tough situations easily. When I started learning that, I came up with my idea of asking myself 'what would a successful guy do?' I thought about putting it on wristbands, WWASGD, but I thought that would be a little much. But seriously, many times I've imagined what a successful guy would do in certain situations and that helps me to look at it differently. And notice I said successful, I want to learn from successful people."

"I see what you're saying, but it still seems so hard."

"Of course it does, El. If it was easy, I would just have texted you how to do it." PJ paused. "Is it too hard?"

"No, no," said El. "I want to do it. It's just new for me."

"Good. Then this is a great place to talk about what to do next." She paused as El stared at her. "El, what action will you take based on what we talked about?"

"Uh, I'm not sure."

"We've discussed the importance of keeping emotion out of it. Maybe you could talk to someone you know who's good at staying calm and not acting emotional."

El thought about her friends and said, "My friend Ann has always been good at looking at problems and taking them apart without getting upset. She's in accounting," she added.

"That's one idea. You could chat with Ann and find out what she does to focus on the task instead of the emotion. Another idea might be to pick something you've gotten upset about and figure out what you could do differently. What else do you think you could do?"

"I'm not sure," El said. "I need to think about it some more."

"That's fine. Decide what action you're going to take and send me a message telling me what you did and how it worked. Then we'll set up our next meeting."

"Uh, okay. What's next?"

"We'll focus on confidence—that's an important part of preparation. Next time, I'll introduce you to a friend of mine who is very confident and she'll share some of her techniques."

More confident than you? El thought but didn't say aloud.

As if PJ had read her mind, she said. "I wasn't always this confident, but I learned what to do to look and sound that way even when I might not feel that way. So El, before we finish up today, do you have any questions?"

Questions tumbled in her brain, but El looked at the time and decided not to ask any. She wanted to try to make the 7 p.m. yoga class, that way she could at least tell Derek she was using the gym membership.

"No, I'm good." She thanked PJ for taking the time to talk to her and said how much she appreciated her help. They chatted for a few more minutes and ended the call.

El stared at the blank computer screen and shook her head from side to side. She wasn't sure what she was expecting, but that wasn't it. She had a lot to think about…and something to worry about. Now she had to do something and report back to PJ. She texted Ann: "May I pick your brain about work?"

Ann texted back immediately. "Sure what's up?"

She could always count on Ann for help.

Chapter 3

"Hey!" El said, when Mr. Fluffy whacked her in the forehead with his paw when the alarm clock buzzed at 5:30 a.m. Mr. Fluffy was not a morning cat. El bolted from bed and stared into the mirror to assess the damage. Her forehead had puncture marks beading with blood. She dabbed at them with a tissue soaked in hydrogen peroxide and said, "Not nice!" to the furry lump on the pillow. At least my bangs will mostly cover the scabs, she thought.

El showered, washed and dried her hair, and swiped her eyelashes a few times with mascara. She then dressed in a forest green sweater and black pants and slipped on black pumps, added food and fresh water to the cat's bowls, packed a lunch so she could tell Derek she did so, and left the house in plenty of time to meet Ann at Starbucks for breakfast at 7 a.m.

Ann was hunched over a laptop in the far corner, fingers flying across the keyboard, *venti* coffee and a chocolate filled croissant at its side. Her hair was blue and spiky today. Her black long sleeve t-shirt dress hit right above her knees and was worn over red and white Pippi Longstocking tights. A red blazer hung from the back of her chair. Ann proudly pushed the corporate dress code.

El admired Ann from the vantage point of the ordering line. She was sure people assumed her 5-foot, funky friend was an art student instead of a mathematical genius who possessed degrees from Stanford and Harvard, and who had quickly climbed to the position of internal audit manager.

When El ordered her soy latte, gluten-free breakfast sandwich, and banana, she joined Ann at her table. It was the first time her friend looked up from the laptop. She squealed. "El. So good to see you," and gave her a hug.

"Thank you for meeting me," El said as they sat down and Ann closed her laptop and slid it into a backpack on the floor near her chair.

"No problem. What's up? You said it was business."

"Yes, I met this woman on a plane last week. PJ is her name and she claims she can help me get promoted." She took a sip of her coffee.

"Does she work at your company?"

"No, I mean, she's like a coach. She's giving me pointers about what it takes to succeed in business. She's a force. A real Wonder Woman. Our age, but way more successful. Or at least more successful than me. She speaks at conferences and…" El wasn't sure what else to add. She took a bite of her sandwich, and then added, "She told me that successful people ask for what they want and they keep their emotions out of it when they do. I thought of you because you're always so calm. I've never heard you complain about work or your boss or raise your voice, and you've been promoted twice since you've started. I want to know how you do it. How can you stay so calm? I mean you have to deliver bad news and people get pissed off. I'd feel attacked and get defensive."

Ann laughed. "That's for sure. I may have one of the most hated roles in the company. Nobody likes to be called on their shenanigans or mistakes. But that's my job, and I kinda love it since it gives me insight into every department in the whole company. And yes, occasionally someone gets in my face and makes an unwise comment, but I don't take it to heart."

"I don't know how you do it. Conflict makes me uncomfortable." El squirmed in her chair just thinking about it.

Ann pulled a piece from her croissant and popped it into her mouth. She drank coffee and then said, "My job is to state facts. Some people don't like to hear the facts, but that isn't my problem. Facts are still facts. They are indisputable. And facts have power and weight. Think about it this way, would you write on your resume that you 'energetically oversaw projects and fulfilled client needs?'"

El's eyes were wide and she shook her head no. "That'd be appalling."

"Exactly. You'd write 'managed 30 client accounts, increased company revenue by x amount of dollars, and designed and implemented a new systems' workflow procedure' or whatever. Facts. No emotion.

That's how I approach each work interaction. Just the facts, please." Ann finished the last of the croissant.

"But don't you ever think things are unfair?"

"Of course. But then I remind myself that I am not always privy to all of the facts. What looks unfair to us may just be our perception because we don't know all of the facts, or it could be that the decision maker also doesn't know all of the facts. I don't know what PJ told you about asking for what you want, but in my experience, facts always support the ask and those facts have to relate to the business. While your boss may care on a personal level that you have bills to pay, for example, the company doesn't really give a shit. The company wants to know how you've impacted the bottom line if you think you deserve a raise. See what I'm saying?"

El nodded, but before she said anything Ann said, "I'll admit that in my head sometimes, if a manager or employee is venting at me, I may be saying, 'Are you done, bitch? Or dude, chill.' It always seems to be women or the young guys they hire fresh from undergrad who are still acting like a big man on campus. But I keep my face devoid of expression and maintain eye contact and eventually they shut up and I resume what I need to say. Staying in a state of calm helps others grow calm, too."

"Very Buddha of you," El joked.

"Don't knock it." Ann grinned. "Try it. You might like it."

"I'll work on it," El said, as she started to collect her empty cup and crinkled her used napkins. "Thank you for meeting me this morning and for sharing that your wisdom."

"Any time. Though next time, let's make it after work and happy hour." Ann pulled on her red blazer and hefted the backpack over one shoulder. In silence, they walked the two blocks to the skyscraper that housed both of their company headquarters.

Shit, shit, shit, El thought. She had started scrolling through her e-mails as soon as she got to work and opened one from her boss, Tom, with the subject line "Office Update." Because of additions to the department…blah blah blah, it would mean "some adjustments in the work spaces"…blah blah and "we'll continue to work as a team" blah blah blah. Bottom line: some new people were being added to her department and some of the group was going to have to move to make space for them. Her name was on the list of people moving. She was being kicked out of her desk and relocated to some bleak place on another floor. She didn't want to move. She liked where she sat and could almost see out of a window if she turned around a little. El didn't think it was fair. Jim didn't have to move and neither did Nancy. They had the cubicles closest to her, and she'd been here longer than both of them.

Ugh! If I move, I won't be able to just walk over and talk to Tom. Not fair at all, thought El. Just wait until she told the girls about this one.

She needed a break to clear her head. She walked down the hall to get some hot water for a cup of tea.

She walked past Leila and Kim. Why didn't they have to move? What had she done wrong? Didn't Tom like her? Maybe he was mad at her for some reason. But why? She paused in taking a step. What if her boss was mad at her? What had she done? Were the people on the list going to be pushed out of the department? Laid off?

She took a breath. It's just a move, she told herself.

Walking back to her desk, she thought, I should text Ann and let her know. What would Ann do? She stopped. Probably not this, she thought. She'd be calm. El sipped at the tea and burned her tongue.

She thought back to what PJ said about things being business not personal. El wasn't sure, but she spent the rest of the morning trying not to think about how much the idea upset her.

But at noon, she gave herself permission to think about it as she ate her salad at her desk while she read and responded to e-mails.

After lunch, she went into a conference room with her laptop, opened a Word doc, and listed reasons why she should stay on this floor. Her first entry was "because it's my desk dammit". She deleted that and thought back to Ann's comments about facts. What were the facts?

The facts were:

1. She had been with the company for two years and they were making her move.

2. Some of the people on the list who were staying in the area had been here less time.

3. She should be consulted before they moved her desk.

4. Moving was a pain.

4. Moving meant that she wouldn't be near her co-workers.

She stalled.

What was really bothering her about this? She didn't want to feel like she was being punished and being sent away. She was afraid that if she moved, her boss would pay less attention to her and she would never get a promotion. She sighed. On the other hand, lots of people would welcome the chance to move away from their bosses.

She stared at the list again and asked herself to forget about the personal. What are the business facts? What are the facts that my boss is going to care about?

She thought about the work she was doing and with whom she was interacting on a daily basis. That made her think about the new project and the team she was going to lead.

She reminded herself a few times to stick to the facts when her emotions felt overpowering. She took some deep breaths and imagined she was Ann. The end result was a short list of factual reasons why it made more sense for El's desk to stay where it was. She circled the top two.

As she walked back to her desk, she saw Tom, her manager in his office. Now or never, she thought. She forced a smile and knocked on his open door. "Hi Tom, do you a few minutes?"

He turned from his computer to her and made eye contact. "Sure, El."

She closed the door and noticed he looked nervous. She smiled, wanting to look friendly. "I just want to check in with you about the planned move."

Tom played with a pen. "El, you know, it's something we have to do. We're running out of space. We need to make some changes."

El looked at his neat desk. No piles of paper or messy stacks of material. The rest of his office looked the same and had minimal furniture. She bet all the files in his drawer were perfectly organized with everything in its place. "Of course," she said, "I understand. There's only so much space, right?"

Tom put the pen down. "Exactly, we have to do something."

"I realize that we have to make moves, but I want us to consider how this will affect the U.K. project."

"What do you mean?"

"You know we're starting this month. It's going to mean that Simon, Kelsey, and I will get pulled into a lot of planning meetings. I know how important this project is." She paused and kept the emotion out of her voice. "The new plan shows me working upstairs and Simon and Kelsey located on this floor. In addition, Suresh is moving to this floor and he will be part of the second part of the project." She took a breath and focused on the facts. "It would make more sense for us to be seated near each other. It'd make collaborating on this project much easier. So I propose that I stay on this floor so I can collaborate on the project with them." She stopped talking.

Tom looked surprised.

"I wanted to mention it because I wasn't sure that the upcoming project was taken into consideration when this was idea was developed."

Tom nodded his head slightly and appeared to think. "Hmm. Of course, this has already been announced."

She had considered this and had prepared her response. "Exactly. That's why this is the right time to discuss it. The announcement gives us the opportunity to make adjustments before the big move. I appreciate you considering my suggestions because I believe it will make it easier for us to keep the project on track. We can't afford to waste any time trying to get the team together."

"Okay. Thank you, El. I appreciate your suggestion."

It's not personal, it's business, she reminded herself and added, "Of course, if it makes more sense for the group to have me move, I will, but I think keeping my desk with the project team would be the best option."

She thanked Tom for his time and left his office. She felt great. She had done it. Even if she didn't get the change she wanted, she had given it her best shot and she did it without getting emotional. She couldn't wait to tell Ann what she had done. El texted: Wanna get happy in an hour?

Ann's response was immediate: I could use a margarita. 5:30 @ Green Gecko?

"CU then," El replied.

For the final hour of the workday, El's heart was happy as she filled out the month's expense report and looked over the slides for the morning's meeting, a follow-up with the company she visited in Florida. Just as she was clearing her desk for the night, an internal message notification appeared on her computer monitor. Tom was asking if she was still there and if she could pop into his office for five minutes.

Her heart raced as she wondered what he wanted, and she automatically thought the worst. "On my way," she responded. She repeated, "It's business. It's business. It's business. Not personal. Not personal. Not personal" like a mantra in her mind,

She took what her yoga teacher called a "deep cleansing breath" to relax her anxiety right before she knocked twice on Tom's open door. He was seated behind his desk, where she had last seen him, though now he had a schematic drawing in front of him. He pushed it towards her as she sat. "This is our floor and all of its cubicles. I thought about what you said. Simon and Kelsey are here." He pointed to two adjacent cubes. "I plan to put Suresh here, in this empty space." Tom pointed to a cubicle across from the others. "And Brittany, who sits here," he pointed to the space next to Suresh's new cube, "is being moved to the fifth floor, so you can stay in your cubicle."

"Thank you," El said, her smile the only sign of the relief and elation she felt. She kept her voice steady as she said, "It'll be useful to have the team together."

"I agree," Tom said, and then dismissed her with, "Have a good night."

El calmly walked to the elevator, but once its doors closed and she was the only one in it, she squealed and wiggled her hips and torso in a happy dance. She couldn't wait to tell Ann.

At 9 p.m. Derek arrived at El's apartment, letting himself in with his key. Mr. Fluffy greeted him with a loud "Meow" and a swat of his paw towards Derek's wool pant leg. Derek bent to the cat's level. "Not the Armani, dude," and scratched the cat's head in the way he loved. Mr. Fluffy purred his appreciation and leaned into Derek's hand. "If only women were so easy," Derek mumbled.

He stood, took off his suit jacket and draped it over El's kitchen chair, loosened his tie and pulled it from his collar as he walked into the bedroom. "Hello, beautiful," he greeted El, who was reading in bed. Her face was clean, her hair was atop her head in a pony tail, and she wore a tank top and flannel pants. She leaned towards him for a kiss. Ann had been so happy for El and her progress that she ended up picking up the tab on their drinks and the super nachos they ate in lieu of a proper dinner. They had a toast to "It's business, not personal" and clinked their cactus-stemmed glasses together, and giggled like the girls they used to be. She couldn't wait to tell Derek, but she knew it was polite to ask about his day before launching into her own.

She closed the mystery novel she had been reading and put it on her nightstand. "How was your day?"

"Exhausting," Derek said. He had stripped to his underwear, folded his clothes neatly atop her dresser, and walked into the bathroom to brush his teeth.

"And your dinner?" El asked. Derek and his partner were courting a Chinese company whose execs were in town. They had spent the last three hours at the hippest restaurant in the city.

"Exhausting and expensive," Derek mumbled over the Sonicare toothbrush's hum.

"Well, I have news." El's excitement made her talk fast and tell a detailed story of Tom's e-mail, her time in the conference room, talking to Tom in his office, and then his giving her what she wanted. By the time she had squealed in delight at what she saw as her almost heroic efforts, Derek had washed his face, peed, turned off the bedroom light, and was in bed next to her.

"Nice," he said. "Though I don't know why you were so upset about moving. It's not a big deal." Then he planted his lips on hers and grabbed her butt, pulling her against him. She was hurt by his comment, but felt celebratory sex would be a good way to end the day so she pushed him backwards so she was on top.

When El's alarm went off at 6 the next morning, she found herself in bed with only Mr. Fluffy. She drowsily looked around the room and into the bathroom. "Derek?" she called.

No response.

"Huh?!" she said aloud and walked barefoot into kitchen to get coffee. She always ground the beans, put water in the reservoir the night before, and set the timer so it would be ready by the ringing of her alarm. A note was scrawled on a piece of printer paper next to the Mr. Coffee. "Hey, hottie. Didn't want to wake you. I have to fly to Taipei. See you next week. Love you. D."

El stared at the note. WTF!?! He didn't tell her he was leaving the country? Who does that? And just as quickly she realized that his visit last night was a booty call. She laughed and grinned. She felt proud of herself for taking charge, asking for what she wanted, and getting her own needs met. Maybe PJ was right. She could get what she wanted if she asked.

She danced with her coffee into the bathroom as the words to Demi Lovato's "Confident" ran through her head. She sang aloud while she waited for the shower water to heat.

She felt like it would be another awesome day.

Chapter 4

That evening, El changed from work clothes to a plain shirt and flannel lounge pants. She ate a salad and was sipping tea as she anxiously waited for PJ's video to show on the screen. She couldn't wait to share her recent office success. Mr. Fluffy was curled in a ball next to her on the couch.

After they had exchanged hellos, PJ, who looked like she had just come from yoga class, and was finally free of the black boot, asked how El was doing and what action she had taken.

El told her about what she had learned from Ann and proudly related the news about the move and how she had handled it.

PJ smiled. "Amazing." They talked about how well it went, and PJ congratulated her for approaching Tom the way she did.

PJ paused. "Tell me what would normally happen in a situation like this? How have you handled it in the past?"

El gave a small laugh. "Oh, I know just what would have happened because as soon as I got the message, my mind started racing and I was already going there. I don't think I would ever have talked to Tom. I would have acted upset at work and complained to my friends."

"Why did you do that in the past?"

El said, "Really, I'd just never thought about it like that. I thought that my feelings were right and it was okay for me to be angry about it, but I couldn't think of a way to say it to Tom that I thought would make a difference." She frowned a little. "And it's not like my feelings aren't valid, it's just that sharing them wouldn't have helped me at work and could have been a problem."

"And next time?" asked PJ.

"First, I'm going to try to stop myself from taking things so personally. When I looked at it logically, it had nothing to do with me. Then, I'm going to take some time and write down the facts. I mean the real facts that the other person cares about. It's only business. Lesson learned. I just need to remember to do it."

PJ smiled again, and repeated, "Lesson learned. Now let's talk about confidence. I'm impressed you already did some of the things that I was going to cover. You were confident enough to get in there and talk to your boss. It sounds like you kept your tone even despite being nervous."

"Yeah, my heart was really pounding," admitted El.

"That's important to remember. You can't always wait until you feel confident to take action. There are certain things you can do to look and sound confident even if you don't feel it. Hold on, I want to text my friend, Shayla. She's going to join us on the call for a few minutes and share her story." PJ quickly texted a message and continued. "It's interesting, if you focus on making sure you look and sound confident, it will help you to start to actually feel confident. It's like your body is telling your brain, 'hey catch up'."

"So fake it until you make it?"

"Not exactly. I prefer Amy Cuddy's version. She's a Harvard researcher with a great Ted Talk about how body language affects how you feel and she wrote a book called *Presence*. She says, 'fake it until you become it.' And I agree. When you act like you're confident, it can help you feel more confident. I know it sounds a little backwards but…"

Another picture appeared on El's laptop screen. "Great," said PJ. "Now you're going to meet my friend, Shayla, and hear what she does." PJ greeted her friend as her face popped up. "Hey Shayla, thanks so much for coming, I want to introduce you to El." Shayla had long straight black hair pulled back in tight pony tail and red-framed glasses that matched the red lipstick on her lips. She smiled broadly. "I'm always happy to help, PJ."

PJ continued. "Shayla is one of the best speakers I've ever seen. I met her at a conference years ago and afterwards I asked her secret because I was scared to death to speak."

Shayla laughed easily and gestured with her hands. "Please. You're a natural."

"But I was afraid," countered PJ. "But it's not about me. Shayla, can you tell El what you do to be confident?"

"You bet. It's funny, El. I still get nervous about every presentation I make. And by now I've lost count how many I've made. And I meet with anywhere from over 7,000 conference participants at a keynote presentation to just one CEO and his five direct reports in a conference room. I still feel butterflies in my stomach but here's one important thing I do: *I don't let that stop me.* I know that nobody can see what's inside my head or what's flitting around my stomach, and I need to focus on what they do see and hear. Now, of course, I know my material inside and out, and I'm always prepared. That's a given. But I need to go beyond that. People need to see my confidence so they believe my message."

She sat up straighter and put her shoulders back. "I pay special attention to my body language. I want to look in charge, attentive, and comfortable. That took some practice. I always stand or sit up straight but not so rigid. It has to look a little relaxed. Frankly, I started looking at a lot of other people to see who looked believable and in charge. What did they do with their hands? How did they hold themselves?

"Then I focus on how I say what I need to say, on my tone. I practice sounding calm and I make sure that my pitch doesn't go up at the end of sentences because that makes it sound like I'm asking a question. I also focus on using strong words. I practice making positive statements and take out any discounters. Do you know what I mean by that?"

El shook her head. "No."

"I take out any language that discounts what I'm saying. For example, I hear a lot of women start off with, 'this may not work' or 'I know we've tried this before but...' and it takes power away from what we say. And then there's my pet peeve. You know what that is."

PJ shook her head, "I'm sorry, I don't know what you mean." She laughed as Shayla groaned. "Yes, I know—it's about saying I'm sorry. El, we tend to say 'sorry' way too much and that comes across as not confident. We may think we're being nice by apologizing, but it doesn't help. Think about it, how often do you start your e-mails with 'I'm sorry'. Now think how often confident people start off with an apology. Of course, if you make a mistake, you should apologize, but I think we do it way too often and when it's not necessary. There are much better ways to start off an e-mail."

El made a mental note to check her e-mails and take out any apologies.

"PJ told me that you want to get a raise at work. When you imagine asking for a raise, what goes through your head? What pictures do you see?"

El frowned. "I don't know. I picture Tom, my boss, not looking very happy."

"That's typical," said Shayla. "We tend to imagine the worst. Now imagine that you're asking a good friend of yours for something really simple. How does that feel?"

El thought about asking Ann for help. "It feels fine. I know that she'll say yes. I don't have to think about it."

"Exactly. So if you believe that your boss will say yes, it's gonna be a whole lot easier for you to be confident about asking for a raise. Here's what I want you to do: I want you to swap your negative mind movie with a positive one. Imagine that you're watching a movie of you and your boss in a meeting. And in this movie, your boss is smiling. You can see yourself talking and you can see your boss nodding and saying yes—"

"But I don't know he's going to do that." El interrupted.

"Of course not, but you don't know he's going to say no, either. And if you believe he's going to say yes, your approach is much different. It's much easier, like asking your friend for something. Feeling confident can come from that positive belief."

PJ interrupted. "That sounds like a good homework assignment to me."

"Okay," said Shayla. "Practice replacing some negative mind movies with positive movies. It will seem silly at first but it makes a big difference in the way you feel. I do that when I speak to large crowds. When I first found out I had to speak to a really large group, over 5,000 people, all sorts of negative mind movies popped up. I imagined myself tripping as I walked onstage, I imagined saying the wrong thing, or having nobody laugh at my jokes. It was horrible." She took a deep breath. "Then I replaced them all with mind movies that showed me looking and sounding great as I start the speech, the audience smiling as

I talked, and everyone looked happy and clapped at the end. I imagine that every time I have to make a speech." She gave more examples and then said she had to go. El and PJ thanked her.

When she left, PJ asked El, "What'd you think?"

"Wow, a lot to think about. She did seem very confident. I'd love to be able to do that."

PJ said, "But El, you've already started. Think about it. When you talked to Tom about the move, what did you do to show confidence?"

El tipped her head to the side and thought. "I took the emotion out of my voice so I didn't show that I'd been upset. And even though I didn't think about it, I slowed down when I talked to him so I sounded calm."

"It also sounds like you used confident language. You didn't apologize for taking up his time or some nonsense like that."

El agreed. She hadn't thought about it like that. "I did at the end say that if I needed to be moved for the good of the team, I would do it. But I meant it to sound like I'm a team player."

PJ nodded. "Hmmm, I'm not sure about that. It depends on how you say it. It could be positive or the other person could see it as a way out and that you're not going to be so upset if they have to say no to you. Don't make it easy for someone to say 'no' to you. But the point is that you got what you wanted so it worked. Do you have any other questions about what we covered today?"

El's head was spinning with information. "None right now, I need to think about this a little more and then I'll probably have some."

"Okay. Let me know what you do with what you've learned and we'll set up our next meeting. We'll discuss building a business case for asking for a raise."

El took a sip of tea. "A business case?"

"Yes, companies don't just give out raises. Why should they should spend more money on you? Next time."

El thanked her. When the call ended she thought about what mind movie she wanted to change. She was in the middle of envisioning an upcoming meeting with the Florida clients, where she was super prepared and walked into the room in her navy suit like she owned the room. The clients gave her their full attention, she was able to answer all of their questions to their satisfaction, and—

Her FaceTime interrupted the movie. She swiped to answer.

"Good evening, beautiful." Derek beamed, displaying teeth almost as white as his dress shirt. His royal blue silk tie made his eyes appear even brighter. Sometimes El gasped at how attractive he was.

"Derek," she almost squealed, which woke up Mr. Fluffy who now was more like Mr. Grumpy, clawing at her and scowling. She was a bit surprised Derek had called, since when he was overseas he rarely did. "Ouch," she said when the cat's nails dug into her thigh too deeply. "Watch your nails."

"Hey, Mr. Fluffy," Derek said. "You should see this hotel." Derek toured his phone too fast around the room for El to get a good look. He walked towards the big windows. "Check out the view." His phone was finally still. She could see Taipei 101, what was once the world's tallest building, trail off into the clouds above.

"Incredible," she said.

"An homage to money." Derek grinned. "I'm at the Grand Hyatt in a suite on the top floor, which seems puny next to that giant. Our first meeting is this afternoon in that building, on the 100th floor. You know it's a financial building, right?" Before she could answer, he said, "And then dinner tonight is at one of the hotel restaurants. Wish me luck. I want this deal."

"I'm sure you'll get it, Derek." He never had any problems exuding confidence and getting what he wanted. El was positive about that.

"Anyway, I just wanted to say I could be back earlier or later than I wrote on the note. Depends what happens in the next 24 to 48 hours."

"Okay," El said. "Thank you for letting me know."

"Scratch the cat for me. Love you." And he signed off before she got the chance to say, "I love you, too."

As El put her phone on the coffee table she thought about Derek. He didn't apologize for running out in the middle of the night. He had called unexpectedly and didn't start with an apology for not setting it up in advance nor did he start with "Is this a good time for you to talk to me?" like she would have asked. He just assumed she was free if she answered, or would state if she wasn't. He always stood and sat upright, not stiffly, but with his chest raised—never hunched over—and if he was ever concerned that he wouldn't get what he wanted, no one ever saw it. Not even her. In the year and a half they had dated he never once mentioned hesitation or fear when talking to someone or going after a deal. She realized he had approached her the way he approached everything in life: sure of what he wanted and that the answer would always be yes, even if he was shot down a time or two first.

She picked up her phone again and texted him. "Random question, but do you see movies in your mind?"

"What kind of movies?"

"Like a preview of a meeting that has yet to happen. Do you envision the meeting with the Taiwanese before you have it?"

"You mean like see myself presenting and them responding?"

"Yes," El texted.

"Not often. But I do make a list of their possible objections so I am prepared to counter them."

"Oh."

"Why?"

"Just wondered."

FaceTime rang again. Derek's brown curls had been freshly combed. "Need to talk about it? I have 10 minutes."

"It's okay. I don't want to take up— El stopped herself. OMG! She was apologizing. She slipped so easily into that mode. "I realized tonight that every time I talk to my boss, or every time before two days ago, I visualized the meeting before it happened and always with the worst outcome."

Derek's eyes narrowed and his brow furrowed. "Why would you do that?"

"I don't know. Nerves. Anxiety. Stress? Asking for things makes me uncomfortable. I'm not like you." Emotions were getting the best of her voice.

"But the only way to get what you want is to ask for it. It's not difficult to comprehend."

"I get it. On an intellectual level. Emotionally, it can be more difficult."

"Practice. In front the mirror if you have to. And stop imagining the worst. The best is just as likely, statistically, to happen."

"Good point," El said. "Thank you."

"I've gotta run," Derek started to say and El interrupted with "Sorry for taking up so much…." OMG, she was doing it again. "I love you," she said as he ended the call. This apologizing thing was hard. She had no idea she did it so frequently.

El found a playlist of Girl Power songs through a Google search on her computer. Of course the Demi Lovato song was at the top of the list. She pushed play. Then El gently pushed the cat off of her lap and walked over to the bottom desk drawer, where she kept old art supplies. She got out construction paper in a variety of colors and glue. She chose red for the background color. And while she sang along to "Confident", she cut out letters in blue, orange, yellow, and green. She arranged them on the red and glued them in place.

When it dried, she used Scotch tape to hang her new "NO APOLOGIES" sign to one corner of her bathroom mirror. There, an everyday reminder, she thought. And she took off her mascara, washed her face, brushed her teeth, and then crawled into bed with the novel she had been reading the past few nights.

El awoke the next morning to a text from PJ. She was going on an unexpected business trip so one of her colleagues in Human Resources would be El's next point of contact for a lesson. El frowned at her phone's screen. She didn't really like HR or find them to be very helpful so she tried to avoid working with them. She was skeptical a meeting with an HR person would be useful. But, then again, El had learned a lot from PJ so far, so maybe she should stay open minded.

As she crawled out of bed, she hit the Girl Power playlist again. It was cued to Raven-Symone's "This is My Time". El listened carefully to the lyrics since the song was new to her. She was particularly drawn to the part that talked about everyone having strength inside them. She restarted this section a few times to learn the words and then danced into the shower while wiggling her butt and singing along.

But when she stepped off the elevator in the office, it suddenly didn't feel like her time. She spied Carl through the open kitchen doorway. El almost laughed aloud seeing his chocolate brown suit. She envisioned it to be the same color as his brown nose. Carl laughed at something someone said. El took a few steps in his direction and saw Tom. That's who made Carl laugh. El felt envious.

"Great job on the Jerome account," Tom said and slapped Carl on the shoulder.

"I told you we'd do it," Carl said.

As El approached the kitchen, Tom said, "Hey, El, Carl and the team solved a big problem for Jerome so they increased their usual order by 30-percent. Isn't that great?"

El forced a smile. "Sure is. Congratulations, Carl." Inside she seethed. Why couldn't she get the accolades? Damn, brown-noser.

"Thanks, El." Carl said, as he and Tom left the kitchen together.

El poured a cup of black coffee and hoped it wasn't as bitter as she felt.

Chapter 5

El went through the motions of her job for most of the day, but she never recaptured the joy and empowerment she felt the few days before. The only highlight had been two texts from Derek. The first said, "Hi, beautiful. Drank too much at supper last night because of all of the toasts." The second said, "But almost have the deal. <3 U."

She was a bit annoyed that he didn't ask about her day, but conceded to herself that he often didn't. After a few minutes of thought she texted, "Good for you." Then she got up, stretched, and walked to the bathroom as a way to take a break and get away from her desk.

At ten to five, she decided she could no longer stand to be in the office so she shut off her monitor, cleared off her desk, and packed up for the evening. She grabbed three tacos from a food truck on her way home, and right after she walked in the door, she fed a bit of the chicken in one to Mr. Fluffy as a special treat.

El decided not to change out of her navy sheath dress when she got home from work, but she did take off her heels. She wanted to make a good impression on PJ's friend. She signed in on time and waited for the meeting to start. A minute later, Isabel Santos joined. Her brown hair was in a pixie cut, and she wore a cream suit jacket over a wine-colored chiffon shell. She looked friendly, unlike some of the HR people that El had worked with in the past.

"Hello, you must be El. I'm Isabel. PJ has told me about you." Isabel smiled.

"Yes, thank you so much for your time, Isabel. I really appreciate it." PJ's response to El's text confirmation agreeing to the change had said that Isabel was the VP of HR at a major consumer goods company.

"Let's jump right in, shall we?" started Isabel. "I understand that you want a raise, and PJ asked me to talk to you about building a business case. Is this correct?"

"Yes, that would be great. I've never asked for a raise before. I've only hoped my boss would notice my good work and give me one, but I found out that isn't the way to get what I want," said El. "So, I want to make sure I do it the right way."

Isabel laughed. "Actually, there's no one right way. There are a lot of different approaches that work but, unfortunately, there are plenty of ways that don't work. I'll tell you what, in my experience, works the best. I view asking for a raise as a business proposition. It's not about you and why you want the money; it's about convincing your boss and the company that it's a good investment for them."

El thought, it's only business.

Isabel continued. "When you want your boss to green light a project, you try to figure out what you need to say to persuade him or her, right? That's what you need to do in order to get a raise. You need to show that spending additional money on you makes good business sense. Think about it, you've got to be really clear about what your contribution is. What do you do that's worth it? And don't assume that your boss knows what you're doing and what your value is."

"But how?" asked El.

Isabel took a sip from a water glass. "What results are you getting that add to the company's profits? How are you making money for the company? Getting a raise is not about how hard you work or the extra hours you put in. It's about your value."

El felt annoyed. She worked really hard and didn't like that Isabel made it sound like her extra weekend hours and late evenings didn't even matter. She knew talking to HR was a mistake. "Can you excuse me a moment, please?"

Without waiting for an answer, El stood up and walked into the kitchen. She grabbed the filtered water pitcher and poured a few ounces into a cup and drank it. She took a deep breath and felt less emotional. She returned to the living room and her computer and sat down.

"Thank you for waiting. But I don't work in sales," said El. "How can I say that I'm making money for the company?" And then immediately she thought of Tom's comment about Carl. That annoyed her even more so she almost missed Isabel's question.

"Do you help support the company to make money in some way? And if you really can't connect what you do to helping make money for the company, then you can think about how you can save money for the company. How do you reduce costs?"

"You're not in sales either. What's your business case? What do you say to your boss?" El said snippily though she didn't mean to take out her frustration on Isabel. But she felt like Isabel didn't care about her hard work.

Isabel smiled as if she appreciated the challenge. "Since I'm in HR, typically, I'm talking about how I help to save money. For example, what I've done to reduce turnover. Having people leave is expensive and the programs I've put into place mean that fewer people are leaving. That saves us hiring costs and training costs when we get people up to speed. I can point to specific things that I have done to save money and that helps the bottom line. I make sure that I quantify what I do. I show my boss the comparison of what we would have spent if I hadn't put the programs in place, what we actually did spend, and the savings difference. Just because I'm in HR doesn't mean I can ignore the numbers," Isabel said.

She sipped water again and then added, "But, for some managers, even that's not enough. They want to know what you're going to work on over the next year. How can you persuade them that your future contributions are worth it? So I also talk about the continuing savings I'm bringing into the company and the upcoming projects that will make a difference."

El thought about the upcoming U.K. project. She was so focused on the project needs that she hadn't considered how much money it could make or save the company. She wondered who on the team could help her with that.

"So El, what example can you think of in the last few months where you made a difference for the company?"

El mentioned a few projects that she had worked on and Isabel asked more questions trying to determine the value. Isabel dismissed the first few ideas with a curt, "Nope." When El mentioned the recent Florida customer problem, the HR VP sounded more interested. "That's something that might work," she said. "Now break it down into some numbers."

El stared off to the right and pursed her lips as she tried to get her thoughts in line. Her annoyance at Isabel and Carl was making it hard to think. It's only business, she repeated to herself.

"There's a customer rating that I developed." She explained how it helped to identify satisfaction of current customers. "Our business is built on repeat business and referrals so I thought it would be a good idea to figure out who is happy and might want other products. It wasn't that hard."

"Really?" said Isabel. "Had anyone else come up with that idea in your company?"

"Well, no but…"

"El, did PJ talk to you about discounting what you do and say?"

El felt like she was back in college, and she had just given the wrong answer to her hardest professor. "Well, yes but…"

Isabel put her hand up to stop her. "No buts. I just want you to hear that you're discounting a great idea you had. I want you to get credit for it. When something is easy for us, we forget that it might be hard for other people. I want you to accept that you did a great job. You're going to need to talk about your accomplishments in a positive way. And horror of horrors, you may need to boast a little," she joked. "But seriously, I know plenty of women who do great jobs and they sit back and don't say anything while other people get noticed and get money."

"But I don't want to be that jerk that's always boasting about the great things he does." El shot back.

"Of course you don't, but you also don't want to be the person who hopes that someone will notice. Hope is not a strategy. It's okay to talk about the great job you do. You need to."

El knew Isabel was right and that it was the same thing PJ had told her on the plane, but was still uncomfortable thinking of bragging.

"Tell me more about this project," Isabel said.

"We looked at the number of customer complaints and what they were complaining about and rated the customers from 1 to 10 with 10 meaning very happy and 1 implying they'll never work with us again. We found that customers in the 6, 7, and 8 categories usually responded well to some additional follow up and tended to buy more products after the follow up." And that's when El realized that Carl and his group just provided more data confirming that. Wow. Maybe his group's success could be a win for her. She liked the sounds of that.

Isabel interrupted her thoughts with, "Do you have the numbers to back that up?"

"Yes, I know that sales were generated after contacting them." El took a breath and then automatically added, "But I didn't have anything to do with the sales."

"No, but that's a great example of something that you put in place to help increase sales. I would definitely talk to your manager about that. How are you letting him know?"

"What do you mean? He knows I did it."

"How many people report to your boss?"

"Nine. Wait, with the changes, I think 11. "

"He's not going to remember everything you do. You need to help your boss know what you're doing. I suggest that you send a brief summary every week or two of the key things you accomplished. That way, he knows. That's where the numbers come in. He might realize that it was a great idea, but does he know that it actually brought in X more dollars last year? That's what he needs to know. That's what he needs to remember when he's considering giving you a raise."

"Oh, I can't do that," said El. "I don't want to bother him."

"I don't look at is as a bother. When my direct reports give me a brief results update every two weeks, I appreciate it. That makes it easy for me to keep track of what's happening."

El frowned. "I never thought about it that way."

"Think about it as how you can help your manager help you. But let's switch gears a little. When does your company normally give raises and promotions?"

"We get our annual increases at the beginning of the year, based on the previous year's performance."

"Not that, I mean when are raises normally given?"

"I think at the same time but also there seem to be some in the middle of the year. We just had two promotions that were announced. I think because there was a re-org."

"There are always going to be off-cycle raises and promotions. But we need to focus on the raise schedule so you can start planning when to talk to your manager," Isabel said.

"Well, if it's not until the middle or the end of the year, I have plenty of time."

"Oh no. You can't wait. If you wait until review time, it's too late. You need to start several months ahead to make sure you're on your manager's mind. Think of it this way: first, your manager can't read your mind. It might be obvious to you that you want and deserve a raise but not to your boss."

El thought about Tom. She'd never talked to him about wanting a raise, but it did seem obvious to her. Who wouldn't want a raise?

"Second, your manager can be your biggest ally, if you let him."

Ally? El had thought of her manager as standing in the way of her raise, not the person who would help her. And yet he had seemed to be chummy with and proud of Carl. Hmm, El tried to picture herself in Carl's place and couldn't do it.

As if Isabel had read El's mind, she said, "Yeah, don't think of your manager as someone that you need to fight against. Most managers want to pay their employees as much as they can. I mean, as long as they're doing the job. But they need to persuade their bosses and HR that their employees deserve raises. That could take some time. Every group has a bucket of money that they use for raises. Why shouldn't you get the money instead of someone in another area?" Isabel drained her glass of the rest of her drink, then continued, "In my company, the managers meet together and pitch who they think should get the raises. Everyone needs to agree. That recommendation gets sent to the senior leaders and HR so we can review it and agree. I've been in plenty of those meetings, and what sets people apart is if other people know them and their results. If the only person who knows what a great job you're doing is your manager, it's going to be hard to get other leaders to agree to a decent raise. But in those meetings, when a manager mentions someone they all know, they can quickly agree."

El started feeling panicky. She didn't know any of the other leaders. She prided herself on getting her job done well and not wasting time on other things. Did Isabel really mean she needed to brown-nose all of the managers, like Carl seemed to do?

Isabel paused, "Questions?"

"Uh, okay. What if the other leaders don't know me?"

"Well I don't know exactly how decisions are made in your company. You should find out. Ask your boss. I do think it's a good idea for people other than your manager to know the great job you've been doing. After all, what would happen if your manager quit tomorrow, and they hired a new manager after he or she leaves? What would your new manager know about you?"

"But how can I do that? I'm so busy with trying to get my job done. I don't have time to just talk to other managers. And even if I did, what would I say?"

"Are you working on any cross-functional teams?"

"No, I don't have time for that." El's brow furrowed; she felt defeated.

"That can be a great way to work with people from other groups and get your name out there. And it doesn't have to take a long time. One year I got volunteered to be on the holiday party committee. I was really annoyed at first and then realized that it gave me a chance to meet new people. It even gave me a chance to talk to the president of the company. I got lots of visibility. You might want to think about some options in your company. But let me get back to raises. In some companies, the raise decision is just made with your manager and his or her manager. As long as your boss's boss knows you and your work, you should be okay."

El was nervous around Tom's boss and hadn't spent much time with him. This conversation was not going the way she had hoped. "But wait, what about salary comparison? I looked online to see how much I should be making and it showed I should get a raise."

"Ummm, maybe. Maybe not. You have to understand that HR doesn't use those surveys. We normally use our own surveys from companies we trust and they don't always match the ones you see online. In addition, we need to pay attention to internal equity, or what other people in the company make. Also, those surveys can have a wide range, so the range of a job could be between $50,000 and $80,000. People look and think $80,000, but that's not what you're going to make, especially if you're newer in the position. Companies don't want to pay at the top of the range because then there's no room for future salary increases. Each company has its own rules about where it'll pay in the range. Some companies focus on closer to the bottom and others focus on the top. It's good to get that external salary information, but don't expect that it's going to get you a raise." Isabel picked up her glass and appeared surprised that it was empty. She set it back on her desk.

El sighed. She had been really excited about the online survey data. "What can I do then?"

"Let's get back to your boss. When you want to persuade your boss and his boss, make sure you know what's important to both of them. What do they care about? How can you help support their goals? Instead of thinking about you, think about them. What's in it for them?"

El had no idea. "How can I find out his goals?"

Isabel waved her hand. "Why don't you just ask him? Let him know that you want to support his goals, that you want to help him. That will make him happy."

El thought about it and said, "Actually, one of the reasons I don't want to talk to my manager about a raise is that I don't want him to be mad at me."

Isabel shook her head. "Let me tell you what really makes managers angry. Managers get upset when someone doesn't ask for a raise, and instead they decide to go look for a job and then they quit. Managers would rather have someone ask for a raise so they have the opportunity to get them a raise if they can. I can't tell you how many managers come in to see me asking us to make a counter offer for someone who has just quit. They're panicking because they want to keep the person. It would save us so much trouble if the manager knew that their employee was concerned about this and had a salary discussion with them before they started looking for another job." She paused. "Of course, you also need to ask in a professional way and I'm sure PJ can help you there."

With the mention of PJ, El asked, "How do you know PJ anyway?"

"She and I used to work for the same company. It's funny, lots of people avoid HR. We get a bad reputation. People are afraid that we just focus on the negative side, such as problems, reprimands, terminations. But PJ saw the other side and asked a lot of questions. Then when she was a manager, she always made a point to get involved and really understand the HR point of view. She is sharp. And she's made a difference in the lives of so many women."

"Yeah, she's starting to make a difference in mine." El sighed. Sticking up for herself and putting herself out there made her anxious. Wasn't there some saying about the rabbit or marmot or something that popped itself out of the hole was the one that got shot? Surely keeping her head down was safer. But she had to acknowledge that it hadn't gotten her very far. She sighed again and realized Isabel was watching her closely.

"You okay?" Isabel had leaned closer to her camera.

"Yes. Just processing and making mental notes of what I need to do next. Thank you very much for your time and insights. I appreciate them." El smiled.

"Feel free to get back in touch if you need more help or a pep talk. And of course, let me know how things go. It's been nice talking to you." Isabel waved.

"Bye," El said and clicked the "end" button.

El felt drained. She walked into the bedroom and changed from work clothes to yoga pants and a tank top. She unrolled her mat in her living room and found a YouTube yoga for relaxation video. If she didn't find a way to quiet her mind, El felt she might go crazy. She sat on her mat with the soles of her feet together. Mr. Fluffy joined her at the top the mat but he was in corpse pose. She laughed. "Silly cat." Then El closed her eyes and focused on breathing deeply, taking long exhales, and summoning her inner wisdom. She was sure it, with help from PJ and her friends, would show her the way.

Chapter 6

After an hour of stretches and meditation with the video and Mr. Fluffy, El felt refreshed and centered. The frustrations of the day had left and in their place were the beginnings of a mental checklist of things she needed to do. And for once, the mental checklist didn't seem intimidating or to induce anxiety. In fact, she was excited about getting started, so she logged into her work's server and checked Carl's calendar. He had nothing scheduled at 8:30 a.m. on Monday so she put herself in that slot, and then she sent him a message: "Will you be in the office at 8:30? I'm scheduling a 30-minute meeting with you then re: your team's recent success."

He responded immediately with "Hey, El. Sure. What kind of coffee do you want? I'll stop at Starbucks on my way in."

El was taken aback. Was he brown-nosing her, too? Or was he a nice guy whose intentions she had misunderstood?

"Tall soy latte, please. Thank you."

If Carl was bringing coffee, El felt it was only right for her to contribute some muffins so she planned to pick some up that weekend to bring with her.

El spent the time before she fell asleep writing in a journal. She wanted a record of what she had been learning from PJ and the others so she could look back from time to time in case she needed a refresher. Though, with luck and practice, the lessons would become ingrained in her actions and viewpoint. And El hadn't forgotten her promise to PJ on the plane: she would eventually need to share what she learned with other women to help them on their own journeys.

1. To get what you want, you must ask.

Besides a raise and a promotion, what do I want? El asked herself. She made a list:

- *To have more than enough money to pay bills*
- *To be debt free*
- *To buy a place eventually*
- *To be recognized for my hard work and accomplishments*

But after El wrote that she heard PJ's voice in her head saying, "Hard work is only recognized when we draw attention to our accomplishments and how we're contributing to the company's success." El sighed. Figuring out how she was doing that was on her mental checklist.

And if El was being honest with herself, she acknowledged that she wanted to feel a bit more central to Derek's life. She hadn't heard from him since the FaceTime calls. No texts good morning. No goodnight messages. No "how was your day?" She didn't even know when he was returning. She sighed again. She loved him but sometimes felt like their relationship was like her work life had been: in a holding pattern and not making any progress towards promotion. They were approaching two years soon. Maybe it was time for her to ask for what she wanted, not just at work, but in every area of her life. For once, that thought didn't terrify El. She felt empowered. And though she felt a bit silly, she put her clenched fists on her hips and assumed the Wonder Woman stance, at least from the waist up since she was seated on her bed with her journal and pen on her lap. "I've got this," she said aloud, and smiled.

Then she wrote:

2. It's business, not personal.

Even things with Derek were a bit of both. If they weren't going towards something, they had no business wasting each other's time, El thought.

3. Stop apologizing and saying I'm sorry.

El grabbed her phone and searched for the screen shot she had saved the day before from a Twitter post. It read, "Replace I'm sorry with thank you. So instead of saying 'Sorry I was late', say 'Thank you for waiting for me.' Replacing negativity with positivity and gratitude breaks the I'm sorry cycle." Powerful, El thought. She was grateful for #twitterwisdom and looked forward to practicing the lesson.

4. Build a business case. Know how you support the bottom line.

That was on the top of her agenda in the morning, and a good place to stop, she realized. She shut the journal and put it on the nightstand and checked her phone one last time to see if Derek had texted. Negative. "Good night, Mr. Fluffy," El said to cat who was curled on Derek's pillow. She turned off the light, knowing she'd make progress towards her raise and promotion tomorrow.

"Blueberry muffins are my favorite," said Carl with a big smile. He handed El her coffee and sipped his. He was wearing red, white, and blue today. Red silk tie, white shirt, and navy suit. El thought he looked sharp rather than ironically patriotic.

El found herself smiling back and sipped the caffeinated ambrosia.

"What can I do for you, El?" he asked.

El had practiced what to say to him and tried to rid her mind of the image of him as a brown-noser. She set her coffee on the corner of his desk and leaned towards him a bit. "Carl, I was really happy to hear about the Jerome account yesterday and I wanted to congratulate you and find out more about it."

His smile broadened. "That's really nice of you but it was the team. They're a great group and everyone pulled together to get it done. They deserve all the credit."

Hmmm, thought El, that wasn't what she expected. "Of course," she said, "but you're the team leader so you made it happen. They wouldn't have been able to do it without you." She leaned back against her chair and picked up the coffee again.

He waved his hand, brushing away her compliment. "They did it. I just made sure they had what they needed."

El asked for more details about the project. As Carl described the progress, he talked more about the value everyone else brought to it and how they all worked together. She was surprised at how little he mentioned what he did. She hadn't talked to him much before this and had expected him to boast more.

He finished his first muffin and then said, "So El, how can we help you?"

"What?" El cocked her head to the side. It was not a question she was expecting.

"What can my team do to support you and your projects? I'm very impressed with the customer rating project and I know you've been a key contributor. It's ground-breaking."

"Really?" She couldn't help herself and asked, "What have you heard?"

"I heard how you were able to pinpoint opportunities with Kelco and Eastern Mountain that helped us beat our quarterly projections by over 17 percent. That was great work. Congrats."

El smiled. "Thanks, Carl, that's so nice of you. I appreciate it. I didn't realize that you knew that much about it."

"Oh yeah, I make it my business to pay attention to projects that I think can really add to our growth." He picked a crumb from his sleeve and then sipped his coffee.

El hadn't thought about the customer rating project in those terms, about how it was contributing to the company's profits. She tore off a piece of a muffin and chewed thoughtfully.

Carl filled in the silence. "In regards to the Jerome project, your ratings project made us see that we needed to spend a little more time with the customer to make sure that they had what they needed. We didn't try to sell them any more products; we just checked in with them and inquired how we could help them use the products that they'd already bought from us more efficiently. Initially, it didn't mean any additional sales, but when they started a new budget cycle, they increased their orders." He paused. "And we're really going to need that to meet our goals for this year."

"What do you mean?"

"You know, the concern about the last quarter's slump."

El remembered the brief mention of missing something at the end of last quarter. But they hadn't emphasized it and she thought of that as something that the executives would take care of. "What about it?" she asked.

"Well, that's one of the things that Tom's working on—one of his key initiatives—how to make up some of that this quarter."

El put the coffee cup down and blurted out, "How do you know that?"

Carl laughed. "I make it my business to help my bosses. That's my job. I look for ways to make sure they meet their goals. I ask people what they're working on and what I can do to help."

"But how do you talk to Tom? He's always so busy. It's hard to find time on his calendar to schedule a meeting. He's always booked."

"Oh I don't always schedule meetings with him. If his door is open, I just stick my head in and chat with him for a few minutes."

El just stared at him. She never considered doing that. She thought she had to schedule meetings to talk to him. He always seemed busy when she walked by his office, and she didn't want to bother him so she left him alone. She hadn't thought it would be okay to just stop in and chat. That's why it was such a big stretch for her when she just went in and talked to him about moving her desk.

Carl continued, "Or sometimes we chat in the break room. Tom's a big football fan and is in a fantasy league and I like to find out how he's doing. And he's training for that marathon so it's interesting to hear about his training."

El wasn't comfortable with small talk with her boss and didn't know what to say when she met up with him in the break room. Now she was embarrassed to think that she hadn't used that time to talk with him. Normally, she grabbed her coffee or tea and fled back to her desk after a quick "How are you?"

"Sometimes Marc joins the conversation. He's not into fantasy football, but his son plays football in college so we talk about the games."

Marc was Tom's boss. El had rarely spoken to him and didn't know he had a son. She found him so intimidating that she tried to keep her distance. She thought about a recent uncomfortable elevator ride where it was just she and Marc. She had frantically tried to think of something impressive to say during the entire ride up to the twelfth floor but couldn't think of anything so she stared at her phone instead.

"What do you say to Marc? He always seems so stressed."

Carl nodded and laughed. "Well you'd look stressed too if you were responsible for making an eight percent increase in revenue. I ask how he's doing, what he's working on, how our team can help. Really, he's just a person. I find most people are happy to talk about what they're working on so I ask about themselves and their projects. I like to get to know people. And try to see how I can help them."

He took a swig of coffee and then said, "So El, what are you working on? How can I help you?"

El thought, you already have. Her head was still spinning from his last comments. She thought back to Isabel's comments about building relationships with Tom and his boss and other leaders.

Aloud, she told Carl more about the customer project and got some ideas from him. They agreed to meet with leaders from some of the other teams to see how they could work together to increase the effectiveness of her project and what everyone else was working on.

El left the meeting and returned to her desk. But before she delved into e-mail and the day's work, she took stock of what she'd learned from Carl.

1. Look beyond your job and see how you can affect the company's bottom line.

2. Ask your leaders what they're working on and help them to reach their goals.

3. Ask your colleagues what they are working on and see where you can collaborate.

I can't wait to tell PJ, she thought. It was only 9:15. She wondered what else she would learn throughout the day. And just as she wondered that a text from Derek appeared on her phone: Hey, beautiful. Miss me? Things are going well here. I'll be staying for another couple weeks to finish the deal and get things set up. Mo' money. Mo' money. Yeehaw.

Do I miss him? El surprised herself when her immediate internal response was no. She was enjoying putting herself and her career first. And even though some of the lessons she was learning and the conversations she was having were uncomfortable at times, she realized at no point since she had met PJ and her colleagues and done the required work did she ever feel put down or insulted. Sure, she had been frustrated or annoyed by what she was told, but no one ever treated her like she was stupid or not their equal. But she had felt this way when Derek talked to her plenty of times. Too many times, if she was honest with herself.

She decided ignoring his question was better than lying, so she texted "Good for you, honey."

Tom's door was open, so before she had time to overthink it and talk herself out of it, she walked over and peeked in. Tom was typing and looked surprised when she said hello. "Tom, I want to check in with you. I just had a great meeting with Carl and have a few ideas about how to meet our goals. Okay if I schedule a few minutes?"

Tom smiled. "Sounds good to me. Anything we can do to move forward would be great."

"Okay, thanks. See you later." That wasn't so hard, El told herself.

Then she checked Tom's calendar and found an open 30-minute slot later that afternoon so she scheduled time with him for a one-on-one. She also searched the calendars for the other project managers in her department and scheduled 30 minutes with each of them, too. She was going to follow Carl's lead and ask them what she could do to support their projects and how they might work together. And then she realized that she might have been wrong about Carl. Maybe all of that talking to his co-workers wasn't B.S.-ing like she thought. It was him taking action, finding out what needed to be done, and how they could all support each other and company sales. PJ's words on their first videoconference came back to her: You need to really understand the situation and the people you're working with so you can help them see that what you want can help them. While El agreed with that, for the first time in her career that she could remember, her focus wasn't on what she wanted, though what she wanted hadn't changed. Her focus was now on her colleagues and Tom. She wanted to find out what they all wanted, what their priorities were, and how could she help, even in that meant more work.

And while she was in that mindset, she crafted an e-mail to her primary contact at the company in Florida.

Dear Suzanne:

I know there's been a lot of back and forth recently and we want to see how we can make the process easier for you. We'd like to see how we can work together and support your use of the products to make it more efficient and effective. May we schedule a call to discuss this?

Thank you for your time and consideration. I look forward to our conversation.

Sincerely,
El Casey

El pushed send, and as she did her cell phone rang. "Hello," she answered.

"Yo, Rella." Her brother Jack was the only one who called her that. "Long time incommunicado."

"Sorr—" She started to automatically say and stopped herself. "Thanks for calling, Jack. What's up?"

Jack was two years younger than El and had dropped out of college after his sophomore year, much to their parents' dismay, to start a food truck. But to everyone's surprise except Jack's, the truck was a hit. Casey's Pit Stop had a huge following and its own app so customers could track where they could buy the BBQ sandwiches and plates they loved. Jack and his truck had been featured on the Travel Channel and the Food Network, and he was even asked to guest judge a cooking competition from time to time. El was proud of her "little brother" who towered over her by six inches.

"Business is booming. Wanna come work for me? I could use another red head around." He laughed. Jack's crew, like so much of the food service industry on the West Coast, came from other places and spoke limited English. But from the time Jack hired his first employee, he bragged to his family about what he learned from them. Hard work, determination, how to never give up, and how to make the juiciest *carnitas* anyone had ever eaten.

"Nah, I'm good where I'm at," El said. "But hey, Jack, when you thought about your business, especially during those first few months, did you ever see yourself failing?"

"What? No. Why?"

"I just wondered." El sighed. Maybe it was a female thing.

"I mean I knew there was a chance I could. You know. But I never dwelled on it. I told myself I had no other option but to succeed, right? I mean I dropped out of school to do this. How bad would it look to mom and dad if six months after I was like, oops, my bad. So success was my only plan." He paused then asked, "You all right, Rella?"

"Yeah. I'm fine. I met a woman and am going through some business coaching, and I realize I have a lot to learn." She absently paged through a few papers sitting on her desk.

"Learning is what life is about. How 'bout if I buy you a cold one tonight and you can tell me all about it?"

"Tomorrow is better, if you're free. Tonight is happy hour with Leticia and Teresa."

"Tomorrow it is. The Gecko at 5:30?"

"Sounds good." After they disconnected, she added it to her calendar.

She spent some time planning what to say to Tom, and when it was time to meet, she grabbed her computer and headed to his office. She was determined to learn about Tom's goals, how raise decisions were made, and what his expectations were for the U.K. project. But right before she stepped away from her desk an e-mail from Suzanne arrived thanking her for asking about their needs, saying no one had ever framed it that way. Could they have a call later that afternoon for 15 minutes? El grinned at the positive reception. "Yes, I'll call you." She typed in reply, before heading to Tom's office.

"Thanks, Tom, for meeting with me on short notice. I've got some ideas for the U.K. project that I want to run by you, but before I do, I want to make sure I'm clear about your goals. What's most important to you about this project?"

Tom smiled and sat back. "That's a great question. Of course we want to make it as profitable in as little time as possible while keeping the customers happy."

El smiled back. "That's our goal. But how are you and the executives going to evaluate this? What success measures should we focus on to help you and Marc meet the goals?"

Tom looked at her. El wondered if she had been too direct. Did that sound like she was trying to suck up? Did she sound too much like Carl? She tried to quiet the voice in her head that was shouting this was a stupid mistake and she should never have listened to Carl. She should just continue what she had been doing before. What made her think this was a good idea?

But then Tom said, "Thanks for putting it that way, El. There are a few things that would be helpful to focus on for me and Marc."

El tried to not look surprised. This might work after all, she thought, and felt a little stupid for doubting.

Tom explained some key indicators that he was responsible for that could be affected by the project. El kept the focus on him and his goals and what she could do to help him. She realized that she'd have to change some of the plans because she'd made assumptions about what should be done. She hadn't thought to ask what was most important to her boss.

Tom also gave her some interesting insight into what Marc and the other senior leaders thought was important. She asked some clarifying questions, but Tom couldn't provide detailed answers.

"We're having a leadership meeting next week and this should be on the agenda. Do you want to come in for a few minutes and ask the group these questions so you can hear directly from them?"

Her immediate panicked thought was, absolutely not. I do not want to talk to them. That is too scary. She thought about how she would have handled this even last week. She would have told Tom that it wasn't necessary for her to be in the meeting; she could give him the questions and he could handle it. Instead she forced herself to smile and said, "That would be great. Thank you for inviting me. Let me know when and I'll add it to my calendar."

They talked for a few more minutes, and El left before her fear took over and changed her mind. She got back to her desk and realized that she hadn't asked him about the raise process. She smiled to herself. That's okay, as there would be time for that in another meeting. She was a bit astounded at how empowered she felt.

Chapter 7

The afternoon call with Suzanne ended up being enlightening. When El had been in Florida with her company's sales rep they listened to Suzanne's co-workers complain about the unreliability of the product's performance. The salesperson and El wondered if somehow the device was faulty or had a manufacturing defect of some kind. They agreed to replace it, but again Suzanne's company complained that the new one didn't work either.

As El listened to Suzanne discuss how they used the device, a precursor to them brainstorming ways the companies could collaborate and make things more efficient and effective, she interrupted. "Hold on! My apologies for interrupting, but I think I know why you're having problems. The primary way you are using the product is an off-label usage."

"Yes," Suzanne agreed.

"I don't think we even considered it being used quite like that. I can check with engineering. In fact, hold on and I'll see if Eric's available and bring him into this call. I'll be right back."

"Okay," Suzanne said.

El put her on hold, was delighted Eric answered the phone on the first ring, gave him a quick update, and he agreed to be conferenced into their call.

"Suzanne, I'm back and Eric Reyes is on the line with me. He was the lead engineer on the development team. Please tell him exactly how you are using the product and what keeps happening."

Suzanne went through the story again and when she finished, Eric said, "If we configure things slightly differently, you'll have much better results."

Suzanne got one her engineers on the line and Eric walked her through the changes. He had them do a few test runs and the device didn't crash any more. He gave the engineer his phone number and said to call if she had any questions.

After the call, Suzanne sent El an e-mail expressing her appreciation. She said she was grateful they had determined the problem and that the fix seemed to be simple. El asked her to keep her posted on the results after they had more real world, off-label usage data. She recognized the possibility of an additional marketing strategy for the product.

El felt like they were finally headed in a positive direction. She started an e-mail to Tom that included an update on that project, but she kept the in her draft folder. She was taking Isabel's advice to heart and made it part of her actions: provide a regular written periodic update to Tom highlighting accomplishments and progress. She would add to the e-mail over two weeks and then send it.

Just then a calendar invite from Tom popped onto her computer screen. He had indeed invited her to the next leadership meeting. The notes line said, "You have ten minutes on the agenda." She smiled at her screen and didn't feel the dread she had earlier. She balled her fists on her hips, nodded her head at the computer, and said, "I've got this." And she believed she did.

At 4:45, after what she considered an excellent, productive day, she left the office. She knew she was leaving a few minutes early but also knew her day started tomorrow with a 7 a.m. meeting with one of her colleagues in London. Leticia and Teresa and she had agreed to meet earlier than usual as they were trying out a new martini bar's happy hour and wanted to make sure they got a table. It had been three weeks since their last get together, the longest they had been apart in years so they had a lot of catching up to do, despite their frequent texts.

Leticia was already guarding a high-top table when El arrived. Her short hair had been cut even shorter, creating an elegant, wavy cap atop her high cheekbones and intelligent, almond-shaped eyes. She was tall, thin, and impeccably dressed, in a way that reminded El of PJ. After they had graduated from the university, Leticia went to law school, worked tirelessly for the first few years, and did so well on a few cases that she was made a partner last year.

Leticia and El embraced like long-lost friends with "great to see you" being exchanged on both sides. Teresa texted that police had an intersection and a sidewalk blocked so she would be late.

"What's good here?" El asked Leticia, knowing her friend thoroughly researched new places.

"Martinis, obviously." Leticia laughed.

"Duuuuh," El said. The drinks menu was extensive, with traditional martinis topped by a plethora of garnishes including house made blue cheese stuffed olives, spicy sausage stuffed olives, and ginger stuffed olives; gherkins; garlic; jalapeno; pimento; cocktail onions; spicy string beans; pickled asparagus; Tomolives; lemon, orange or lime slices; or a lemon twist, and new martinis that sounded more like dessert like such as Almond Mocha, and something that was served with a garnish of Gummi Bears. The food menu looked less inspired. "Is the food edible or awesome?"

"Mixed reviews," Leticia said, while making eye contact with a man at a corner table who wearing a fitted charcoal suit and some killer blue suede shoes. He looked a lot like Taye Diggs. "The house made chips are supposed to be delicious and the cheese and charcuterie tray. But you know Teresa won't eat that." She grinned at the man.

Teresa was vegan. El watched the man smile back. He said something to his companion and started towards them. "Hell, no. Three weeks we haven't seen each other. You can't ditch me."

Leticia laughed. "Promise I won't, but ooooh, baby."

"Agreed." El signaled to a waitress. "I'll order us the chips and the blistered shishito peppers with sea salt. What do you want to drink?"

"Whatever," Leticia said with a wave of her hand. Her attention was focused on Mr. Handsome, who was introducing himself as Jackson. He shook hands with both of them. "May I buy you ladies some drinks?"

"Actually, it's girls' night," Leticia said. She placed a hand on his left forearm and leaned closer. "But I would be interested in getting a drink with you either later tonight or Friday, if you're free." As the words were leaving Leticia's mouth El suddenly realized Leticia was a pro at asking for what she wanted and getting it. She almost missed Jackson's first words as he said, "A woman who is loyal and isn't afraid to say what she wants. I like that." Jackson used his right hand to pull out a light grey business card from his inside suit jacket pocket. He handed it to Leticia. "Drinks and dinner on Friday. Six good for you? Text me tomorrow morning and I'll tell you where to meet me." He gazed into her eyes for two beats and then went back to the corner table and his friend.

Leticia looked at El and then down at the card. "Did that just happen?"

"Absolutely. And good for you. He is so hot."

"Jackson Trey Huber III. Seriously. One fine looking man."

As their food and drinks arrived so did Teresa, who after hugging them both, immediately launched into complaints about the police shutting down the street for something, followed by how angry she was at her boss for not giving her enough work to do. El started to murmur support, but then silenced herself. Why couldn't Teresa see opportunities and create her job? She ended up asking that aloud, which stopped Teresa's mouth moving.

"Huh?" Her head jerked so hard towards El that Teresa's three-foot long braid swung.

El signaled the waitress for another round of drinks and explained, "Remember I texted you about PJ, the woman I met on the plane, who, along with some friends of hers, have been mentoring me about how I can be more successful at work? One of the things I've learned is how important it is to find out what matters to your boss and your boss' boss. What are their priorities? What are their needs? And then, if you create a way to help them reach those things, you all win, and you might be promoted.

"Take Leticia for example, she knew winning cases was important to her bosses and the firm. And she knew how important research is towards winning cases. That's why she not only worked her ass off but worked smarter than other people...and was made partner before some of the people she started with."

Teresa said, "Leticia got promoted because she is awesome. Everyone knows that."

"True," El said. "But she works smart not just hard. If you're saying you don't have enough work to even work hard then I think you should find yourself some work to do. Ask your boss what's important. I did that today and was surprised how open and talkative Tom was and it was barely even scary. And guess what? He invited me to the senior leadership meeting next week and gave me ten minutes on the agenda to ask the senior leadership what is important to them and how I can help support that. Isn't that great?" El grinned.

The waitress put the drinks on the table and Teresa lifted her glass. "To El's success." They clinked glasses, drank, and then she said, "You need to tell us more. What else have you learned?"

El said, "I will but before I do that, see that super hot guy in the corner with the fancy shoes?"

All three of them looked over at Jackson, who nodded his head towards them and smiled.

"He's taking Leticia to dinner on Friday. You missed that because of the police detour." El bit into a pepper and this one was hotter than the rest. Her tongue felt fiery.

Teresa started to curse the detour again, but El cut in changing the subject. She wondered if that's how she used to sound when she complained to the girls, to Derek, to PJ on the plane. If so, she'd need to stop that. She now found it uncomfortable to listen to.

Leticia smiled as she picked up her drink and said, "Sometimes you've just got to go for it. Okay, dish. What happened that started all this?"

El thought about what PJ had originally told her, that she needed to share what she learned with others. She took a breath. "Well it started like this…" She told them about meeting PJ on the plane and asking for her help. "That's when I started to realize that even though I thought I was asking for things before, I really wasn't clear. I was hinting and hoping. You have to really say it and tell people even though it seems really obvious." She smiled at Leticia. "Like with Mr. Handsome over there. You made it very clear what you wanted." Leticia threw back her head and laughed. "Oh yes, I'm good at that."

Teresa frowned. "Okay, that's great to get a date but not for work."

El looked at her friend. "Why not?"

"I can't just ask my boss for things. She's not going to give them to me."

"I thought the same thing, but what I'm realizing is that it's not all about me. I have to show them why giving something to me is good for them." She thought back to Carl. "And to do that, I need to understand what's important to them, what worries them, what their goals are. Then I need to show them how I can help. Remember Carl?"

"Ugh, Mr. Brown Nose?" said Leticia.

El briefly felt badly about how much she had complained about him to her friends. "Well, it turns out he's not so bad." Both Teresa and Leticia made faces. "No, really," said El as she told them what she had learned from Carl. "And that's how I got the idea to talk to Tom. And I now I have a meeting with the leaders next week."

Teresa made another face. "Why would you want to do that? That sounds awful."

El paused, thinking that a few weeks ago she would have said the same thing. "I want to help Tom and I want to increase my visibility. When they make the raise decisions, I want them to know who I am." She talked about the meeting with Isabel and how she had explained how to get a raise from an HR perspective.

"Because it all comes down to the fact that I need to make more money, ladies, otherwise I will not be able to enjoy nights out like this." She raised her glass. "To getting paid what I'm worth."

Leticia and Teresa raised their glasses. "Yes," said Leticia. "Sounds good," said Teresa, "but I still don't know. It seems like a lot of work."

El laughed. "You were just complaining that you didn't have enough work to do. Here's more work that you can do that will actually help you."

Teresa nodded and smiled. "You got me. Tell me more."

El talked about some of the other key things she had learned so far. She mentioned the importance of not taking things so personally and viewing getting a raise like a business project and how to build a business case that shows value and connects to leaders' goals and the bottom line. Teresa snorted at that, but El kept going.

She told them about the office move and how she didn't want to get stuck on another floor. She looked at Teresa as she admitted how she would normally handle it by sulking at work or by complaining to them.

Her friends laughed and Leticia said, "Any time, girl, any time."

"Yeah, it's great to know I can," said El, "but that wouldn't fix the problem." She explained how she calmly talked to Tom and made her case about the project and not about how she felt. When she described how she got what she wanted, her friends raised their glasses. "To El!" they cheered.

El said PJ helped her to realize how many times she was saying "I'm sorry" in her conversations and her mails. And with Derek, she silently added to herself.

She talked about PJ's suggestions about the importance of showing confidence and tipped her glass toward Leticia. "And I'm going to learn more about that from you." She suddenly felt like she had been monopolizing the conversation. "So teach us, wise woman. What's new with you?"

Leticia told her friends about her latest case, how she was handling working with one of the new partners, and recent issues with a co-worker.

They ordered more food and Leticia turned to El and said, "And you, what's happening with Mr. Cute? You haven't mentioned him yet."

El paused. True, she hadn't mentioned Derek at all. She briefly told the story of his recent travels and ended with, "so I'm not sure when he'll be back."

Her friends looked at her. Leticia raised her glass. "Here's to men. You can't live with 'em..."

"You can certainly live without 'em," finished Teresa. The friends laughed.

Leticia looked at El. "Seriously..."

El raised her hand to block the discussion. "I know, I know. I don't want to go there tonight."

Leticia nodded. "Noted. Okay, on to other things. Teresa, what about you? What's your love life update?"

Teresa laughed. "I wish this guy named Jordan would call me..." She launched into a story about a guy she had met at her cousin's wedding.

At one point El interrupted after Teresa's third or fourth "I wish." "We don't get things by wishing, dear friend. That's one thing I've learned these past weeks. We get things by taking action."

Teresa looked worried.

Leticia cut in with, "So, besides Facebook stalking him and staring at your phone wishing for it to ring, what other actions can you take?

And no, asking your cousin and her new husband if Jordan has asked about you isn't a positive action either."

Teresa laughed nervously and quipped, "Middle school was long ago."

"Exactly," Leticia said.

El asked, "Do you have his number?"

"Yes." Teresa pulled her phone from her purse, opened her contacts, and showed her friends where he added his number. He had even put "From Rico's wedding" in the "company" line.

"Have you called or texted?"

Teresa shook her head no. El teased, "It is not 1940. You can call a boy."

"Give me that phone." Leticia plucked it from Teresa's hand. She opened the message app and typed "Jordan" so that his phone number popped up. Then she said, "How about 'enjoyed dancing with you. Let's do it again sometime'?"

Teresa said, "Ummm, I'm not sure."

El said, "No, too vague. It sounds like a hint. Asks in business and our personal lives should be specific. 'Enjoyed dancing with you. Want to do it again this Friday night?' would be better."

Teresa was squirming in her seat. "Guys, the only time I've ever been this forward was back in college when I was drunk."

Leticia laughed. "Friend support is better than liquid support."

"Absolutely," El said. "Though right now you kinda have both." They all laughed and raised their half empty martini glasses. "So are you free Friday night, if we're asking him out for you?"

Teresa admitted to having no plans, and added, "The idea of him saying yes is giving me butterflies, but what happens if he says no?"

Leticia said, "Then El will take you dancing. Right, El?"

"Exactly. So it's a win-win. You go out with him or with me since Leticia has a date."

Teresa grinned and drained the last of her drink. "Okay. Then let's do this." She took her phone back from Leticia and typed "Enjoyed dancing with you at the wedding. Want to dance together again on Friday night?" She pushed send and all three of them stared at the phone screen.

Within seconds was a response. "Yes. Out now with friends. I'll call you tomorrow."

Teresa squealed. "I love you guys." She group hugged them.

"See, actions are better than wishes," El said. "And we expect texts tomorrow with an update after he calls."

El pulled out her own phone and went to her Girl Power play list. She showed it to her friends and said, "I've been listening to this for a few weeks now, especially as soon as I wake up each morning, and doing the Wonder Woman stance." She showed them what she meant. "I'm not sure why it works but it does make you feel more empowered. Leticia, I know you don't need this as you're the embodiment of empowerment, but Teresa, you're more like me. I'm sharing the play list with you..." She messaged it to her. "...in case you want to try it and see what it does for you."

Leticia said, "Hey, send it to me, too. I love some of those songs."

"Thanks, El," Teresa said. "I'll give it a try."

At that they decided to wrap it up. El was thrilled to spend time with her friends but she admitted to herself that the evening lasted too late, especially since she had a very early morning. El was beat when she got back to her apartment. Mr. Fluffy was not amused and loudly complained that his food bowl was empty.

As she removed her makeup and washed her face, El briefly checked her messages and saw a meeting invitation from PJ. She accepted and sent a brief update to PJ of what she had done. She was looking forward to their next discussion. But first, she had six hours to sleep before her alarm went off at 5 a.m. and kicked off a very long day tomorrow that would end with what she was sure would be an entertaining supper with her brother.

Chapter 8

El's alarm blared "Run the World (Girls)" by Beyoncé, which caused Mr. Fluffy to swat at her with his paw. She was thankful he missed and hit her pillow instead of her face. Despite the lack of sleep, El felt energized. Evenings with her best friends often made her feel that way. And she was sure today would be another productive and incredible day. She dressed in her favorite evergreen knit wrap dress and added the emerald drop earrings that were Derek's birthday gift to her last year.

She grabbed a Greek yogurt, some granola, and fruit to eat breakfast at the office and threw together a salad with dried cranberries and walnuts for lunch. She changed Mr. Fluffy's water and added some food to his bowl, and was out the door and in the office by 6:45 a.m.

Yesterday, in her flurry of scheduling meetings, she had scheduled the call with the people in the U.K. to talk to them about their expectations for the project. El thought the best way to effectively lead the team and get the desired results was if they all knew what the expectations were from the beginning, from management, from the client, and from each other. She planned to ask a few questions and listen and write down the answers so she could discuss them with the team during their first meeting.

The meeting only lasted 30 minutes, but by its end, El had a clear understanding of the client's expectations, and she learned a little about them, too. She was looking forward to working with them and told them that and that they'd be in touch as a whole team shortly. She thanked them for their time.

Just before 8, Tom sauntered by her cubicle and stopped when he saw her. "You're in early. Trying to get a worm?" He joked.

"I prefer yogurt and granola to night crawlers. I had an early meeting with the U.K. client before their day ended. Are you headed to the kitchen? I could use some more coffee." She grabbed her empty mug from her desk and followed Tom towards the kitchen.

El thanked Tom again for inviting her to the leadership team meeting and for giving her ten minutes on the agenda. She briefly filled him on the progress that had been made in Florida. He seemed interested, which made El feel at ease.

They walked back to their area and El paused at Tom's door. El thought, now's as good a time as any. "Tom, do you have a few more minutes or do you need to get to a meeting?"

Tom chuckled. "No, I have a little time to enjoy the coffee before my next meeting. What's up?"

El followed him into his office and sat down. She realized that she probably should have thought of what to say. "I'm interested in understanding the raise process better. Can you tell me how raises are decided?"

She was worried that Tom might be annoyed, but to El's surprise, he smiled. "Thinking ahead. Good idea. I think planning is very important. Once a year, the company decides on a raise budget. That gets broken down by each department and then each group gets a bucket of money. The compensation team provides guidelines which we use to decide how we're going to spend the money. All the managers, including me, put together our recommendations. These are reviewed by an executive committee to make sure they agree and they follow the compensation guidelines."

"I see," El said. She wondered how much influence the managers had. "I know when the raises are given, but when does the executive group meet?"

"About six weeks or eight weeks before," Tom said. "I know last year your raise was barely above the cost of living increase. That's why I've been giving you a few more high-profile assignments. Show us what you can do, El, in the months that are left." Tom smiled, and El felt her heart race at the encouragement. Admitting he gave her more high-profile assignments was the biggest compliment Tom had ever given her.

She thanked him for the opportunities and with "Run the World

(Girls)" in her head she asked, "Tom, what should someone do to make sure they're considered for a good raise increase this year?"

"Keep doing what you're doing. I believe the U.K. project is going to be key for us this year. Keep supporting the sales groups and help them understand the customers better so we can increase sales." He sipped the coffee. "But El, I want to be clear. I expect that raises will be at the same level as last year. The company is doing well, but it's a difficult market out there. Of course, you know I'll do the best I can for my team, but I want you to be realistic."

El forced a smile. "Of course, Tom. I get it. I appreciate your help." She ended the meeting and walked to her desk.

Ugh, she thought as she tried to clear her head. She didn't know what to think. When he mentioned the high-profile projects, that sounded promising, but then he said that she should expect a small raise. She shook her head and looked at the rest of her day's schedule to help get her back on track. Her 20-minute check in meeting with PJ was scheduled during lunch. She had booked a conference room for privacy. She wondered if she should reschedule. She wasn't really in the mood to discuss raises today after talking to Tom. And if raises were going to be small and wouldn't be decided for a while, why should she spend time on it now?

She reluctantly started reading her e-mails to at least feel she was getting something done. Derek had sent her an e-mail. It was a forwarded article on Refinery29.com titled, "How I went from a $33,000 a year salary to a $185,000 one." The woman in the example was 29 years old and worked in marketing and project management and lived in the same area El did. Derek's comment was "This could be you, babe."

Not likely, was her first thought. And she was annoyed at Derek as she couldn't figure out if he meant to be encouraging was criticizing her for not being that woman. But once she pushed her emotions aside, she realized the woman in the article had done just what PJ and her friends were telling El she had to do: she very specifically asked for what she wanted and made sure she was visible to top management and gave them exactly what they wanted and needed workwise. The woman was persistent and didn't let "no" stop her in going after what she wanted. El bet she wasn't running around saying "I'm sorry," all of the time either.

She sent Derek a short response. "That will be me soon. Thank you." She thought that answer was more in line with Amy Cuddy's "fake it until you become it" philosophy, and El felt proud of herself for not getting trapped in fear mode.

At lunch time, she grabbed her salad and settled into the conference room. She felt odd talking to PJ from the office but decided that the mentorship was helping her with her job.

She took a deep breath and dialed in. PJ joined a few minutes later. El admired her well-cut jacket and matching accessories – elegant and understated, once again.

"How are you doing, El?" welcomed PJ. "That green is a great color on you."

"Thank you. Not bad and how about you?"

"I'm great! I loved your last message. Very impressive. I'm pleased to see that you're taking action."

El perked up at the compliment and thanked PJ.

"I think it's great that you actually met with Carl and decided to listen to him. Even if you don't like him, it seems like you can learn from him," said PJ.

El laughed. "Actually, he's not so bad. I realized that part of the reason I didn't like him was that I was jealous. He seemed to be getting a lot of recognition and I wasn't. Now I realize that he focuses on understanding what other people want and helping them get it. He offered to help me with my project. Of course, he'll get something out of it also."

"I'm sure he will," said PJ. "Tell me what else you've done."

El made a face. "Let me tell you what happened today. I thought things were going well and this happened." She described the conversation she had with Tom.

"What's the problem?" asked PJ, frowning.

"He said raises will be the same as last time. What's the point of spending time on this when I'm just going to get the same amount I got last year?"

"Well, if you really believe that, you're right. Let's not waste any more time." She paused. "On the other hand, if you believe like I do that everything is negotiable, then it's a great time to keep going. What do you think?"

El started to apologize and caught herself. "Yes, I'd like to keep going. It was just disappointing."

PJ brushed it away with one of her manicured hands. "It's a bump in the road and not even a big bump. First, you're assuming that just because general raises are going to be the same, that means your raise could be low…"

"But Tom said…"

"Tom knows he can't promise you anything right now. He doesn't want you to get disappointed if he can't get you more. Second, that's how things normally happen, but there are always exceptions to the rules. Sometimes there is a discretionary bucket of money for high performers. Third, even though you may understand the basic raise process, there are always raises and promotions that happen at different times of the year. Didn't you mention that there had been some recent promotions?"

"Sure, because of a recent reorg."

"See," said PJ. "You could get a raise or promotion at any time. Now, let's get back to what you said to Tom. What specifically did you say to him about getting a better raise?"

El felt nervous. "Well, I realized I probably should have planned what to say. I just took the opportunity and if I'd thought about it, it could have been better."

"Don't worry about it. You took the chance to say something and that's a start. Let's use it and build on it for the next step."

"I said something like 'what should someone who wants to get a better raise do?' I felt funny about saying I want a bigger raise so I made it a little more general. He got the message though," she added. "And he talked about what I could do with my projects."

PJ nodded. "Okay, good start. Now, it's time to talk about how to clearly ask for a raise. The first thing you need to do is set a good tone. I think you've been doing well with that, for example your request about moving the desk. You were positive, relaxed, and open.

"The second step is to clearly ask for what you want. I think this is something to work on. You've mentioned that you want a raise and a promotion. What do you really want now?"

El thought about it for a few moments and PJ watched her in silence.

"Hmm, I've been so focused on the money that I haven't really been thinking about the promotion. I do think I should get a promotion, too. I've seen other people get promotions and I think I deserve one."

"What are they doing that you're not?" asked PJ.

El shrugged. "That's the million-dollar question, isn't it?"

"What can you do to find out? Here are some things to think about. What's their scope? People who are responsible for bigger teams or projects or larger customer bases tend to get promoted. What's their responsibility? People higher in the organization tend to have more responsibility for higher revenue results or budgets. And of course, there's visibility. You can have all these things, but if no one else knows, you won't get promoted."

El thought about it. "I need to think about it and look into it more. I just don't know."

PJ smiled. "That's a great homework assignment. Decide exactly what you want to get and we can work on how you can clearly ask for it and get it."

El nodded and said she would.

PJ changed the subject. "What have you been doing to share the information with others?" El described how she talked to her friends about it. As she briefly mentioned the conversations, she thought about Teresa and she promised herself to check in with her as soon as they were done with this Skype.

El thanked PJ for her help and they chatted for a few more minutes. After the call ended, El stayed in the conference room and slowly ate her salad, thinking about her next steps. She texted Teresa: Are you at lunch too? If so, did he call?

And then she realized that Jackson said he'd call Leticia about where to meet for him for drinks and dinner so she copied and pasted her message to Teresa in a message to Leticia.

Leticia responded first, and when she said where they were meeting, El remembered the place being named the top sushi restaurant in the city. Its sake by the bottle list was extensive and its menu was *prix fixe*. El wrote back, "How did he know sushi is your favorite?"

"He asked what kind of food I wanted. I told him. He must know someone. The wait list to get in there is at least a month long."

And once again El realized Leticia got what she wanted because she asked for it. "So happy for you," she texted in response.

"Me too. LOL," Leticia said.

Teresa texted El, "Sorry for the delay. Yes. I'm meeting him for tapas at 7:30 followed by dancing."

El wrote. "No sorry. Don't apologize. And woohoo. See, we can get what we want with a specific ask."

"I guess. Can you help me pick out an outfit?"

"Yes. I'll FaceTime you tonight after I meet Jack for a drink."

"Oooo, how is tall, red, and handsome?"

"I'll let you know tonight. Back to work for me."

"Okay. Xoxo."

El left the conference room and returned to her cubicle. A very small bag of catnip was sitting on her desk with a Post-It note. "Free sample from the pet store one block north. Carl." El wasn't sure what to make of it so she made her way to Carl's office. He was staring at a blank Word document on his computer screen, his fingers poised but still, over his ergonomic keyboard.

"Knock, knock," El said.

He grinned when he saw her. "I heard you had a cat."

"You heard correctly. Mr. Fluffy will be euphoric. Thank you."

"I walked to lunch and they were handing out the samples and originally I planned to just say no. But then I thought, wait El has a cat. So I said yes to the sample."

"And here we are." El laughed. "That was very nice. Do you have a minute?"

Carl waved towards his open guest chair. "Please. Sit."

"I've been thinking about the things you said. You asked what you could do to assist me and the projects I'm leading, but what can I do to assist you, Carl? You just got that promotion and so I assume you have more responsibilities now. How can we help you?"

Carl grinned. "Thank you, El. Yes, I did get a promotion and I'll be taking over some new special projects. Promotions are funny, you know? Sure, they are based on work and results you've gotten but they also have to do with potential, too. My new role is one I'll be growing into, so at the moment it is all so new I don't know what help I'll need. But I'll keep you and your teams in mind as I figure it out. Thank you, El."

"Thank you, Carl, for keeping me in mind, and for the catnip." And she thought, for the insight. She inadvertently had done her latest action from PJ. She stood to leave, but Carl said, "Is your phone with you? I'd like to see a photo of Mr. Fluffy. I love animals but am hyper-allergic to cats."

El flipped through the first five photos of Mr. Fluffy that she found on her phone. Carl ooooed and aaaahed over the feline's exquisite coat and expressive face, then he thanked El, and returned to the blank Word document and started typing.

El returned to her desk, set up a meeting with her U.K. project team for late the next week, and spent the last few hours of the work day reading background materials on some of the companies she'd be working with on upcoming projects.

At 5:30 sharp she walked into The Gecko and found her six-foot tall brother waving his arms over his head shouting, "Rella, over here" to get her attention. El chuckled to herself and thought, like he needs to do that for me to find him. In a sea of suits and business dresses, her brother stood out for his wavy red hair and his denim shirt left untucked over khaki jeans and burgundy boot attire. He scooped her into a bear hug and twirled her around.

"Put me down, you nut." El laughed.

"Your wish is my command, mi-lady," and he planted her butt on the barstool. "What's your liquid poison? They have some new craft beers on tap."

Once they ordered their drinks and the stuffed jalapenos appetizer Jack wanted to try, along with guacamole and salsa for the chips, and a Cancun salad with marinated shrimp and mango for them to split, Jack took a moment to thoughtfully regard his sister. "So Rella, what's with the failure question? What's going on with you and what is that woman who's coaching you telling you to do?"

El laughed. "The failure thing is all me. Or was all me. I was feeling defeated and complaining way too much, especially to Leticia and Teresa—both of which say hi, by the way—and to Derek. But I couldn't see that I was doing that or that there was another way, or that getting what I want was even possible."

Their drinks and chips arrived so El took a breath.

Jack said, "There are always other ways."

"I know that now," El raised her beer in a toast. "To perspective."

"And to learning and change," Jack added.

"Here, here." El said and then took a sip. "Oh this is the best gluten-free beer I've ever had." She had ordered a dark beer with coffee overtones. It was rich and one sip made her insides feel like they were relaxing.

She spent the next fifteen minutes bringing him up to speed on meeting PJ, all of the meetings with her and her friends and with Tom and Carl. He nodded and said "good for you" a few times but mostly listened. When she stopped, he said, "Rella, you know the most important I've ever learned and it certainly wasn't taught to me in school. It's this: every single encounter we have, with strangers, acquaintances, friends, colleagues, even people we hate or hope to never see again, they are all learning experiences, but it is up to us to look for the lessons and then apply them. I learn from my customers. I learn from the complainers and trolls. I learn from my employees and from our vendors. I would never be successful if I didn't have so many teachers.

"I'm so glad you found this PJ woman to teach you. She sounds like quite a success. You said she's our age, right? Is she single?" He raised an eyebrow and smirked at her.

El laughed and smacked his bicep. But then she admitted that she's never asked about PJ's personal life and it had never come up.

"Maybe you could poke around a little for your charming, successful bro." Jack wiggled both eyebrows at her.

"Hmm, not sure. Are you the love 'em and leave 'em type?" El took a bite of shrimp and mango together and loved the combination, with its kick of red pepper. "Mmmm," she said.

"I was," admitted Jack. "And I've learned from it. I don't need a playmate. I need a collaborator, a co-conspirator, if you will." He winked at her.

"Oh yeah, and what are you conspiring?"

"To take over the food truck kingdom, of course." He popped a stuffed jalapeno into his mouth, chewed slowly, and swallowed. "We should add these to our menu."

"I thought you already were the food truck king, Jack. I'm sure I've seen the crown." El flashed him a toothy grin.

"You have mango in your teeth," he said, which made her cover her mouth with hand, and pull out her phone to reverse the camera so she could see. "Made you look," Jack taunted, just like when they were kids.

"Jerk," she said, laughing. "Some things never change no matter how much we grow and age."

"I'd hope not," he said. "But more seriously, I want a woman to be my queen and rule and expand the food trucks with me. I have ideas beyond barbecue. We could have smoothie and juice trucks that could go every day to that noon free yoga in the park. And maybe a dog-centric truck could go between the dog parks and dog beaches and popular hiking spots and sell treats and that newish rehydrating sports drinks for dogs, poop bags, and dog-lover themed snacks and beverages for humans. I have all kinds of ideas."

El loved her brother's enthusiasm and the fact that he was always generating ideas to expand what he was doing. PJ just seemed a bit more stylish and sophisticated, from what El had seen. But who knew. "I love the possibilities," she said, while eating the last of the peppers.

"That's the second most valuable lesson I've learned," Jack said, signaling for a second round of beer. "Every moment of every day, be open to possibilities. With everyone you meet, in every circumstance. You never know where or when the next awesome idea will come, and it only takes one opportunity to change the course of your life."

"That's true." El said. "I can't believe how much my life has changed in a short time because I sat next to PJ on a plane." And then she realized she was living her brother's first most valuable lesson: she was learning even from him.

Chapter 9

El texted Teresa when she got home and they Face-Timed. Teresa pulled dresses out of her closet as El watched. "Ugh," said Teresa, putting a pale pink dress back into the closet. "I don't have anything to wear." She shook her head. "Maybe I need to go out shopping, get something new."

"Whoa," said El. "You have plenty of nice things. What about that purple dress? Or the black and white top?"

"Maybe you're right. Maybe a dress is too fancy. Maybe I should be more casual." She fell back onto the bed. "This is just too hard. I hate going out on first dates."

El decided she needed to stop this. "Hold on, this isn't like a first date. You already danced with him at the wedding."

"True," said Teresa, as she pulled out some shirts from a dresser and put them on the bed.

"Tell me about him. What's he like?"

Teresa smiled and tipped her head to the side. "Well, Jordan's really cute. Nice brown eyes and great smile. He's a high school English teacher. Super nice." She paused.

"Why was he at the wedding? He's not some sort of long-lost cousin of yours, is he?" teased El.

"Ewww, no. It was my cousin Karine's wedding and he's a friend of her new husband, Rico. I think they went to school together." Teresa paused again. "He's nothing like Neil."

El thought about Teresa's ex-boyfriend. They'd been together for almost four years and had only recently broken up when Neil declared that he needed some "space". Teresa wouldn't say much about it at first, but later she had cried over him one night over drinks. She said she didn't know what she had done wrong. When he said he wanted to talk about their relationship, she thought he was going to finally start to discuss the wedding she had been dreaming about.

El looked at Teresa's smile and was glad she was going out dancing.

As they reviewed outfit options, Teresa told El more about Jordan. As they talked, Teresa decided on a blue dress with black accents and some black heels.

El said, "He does sound really nice. You deserve someone to treat you well. You're an amazing person and you need to spend time with a guy who can really appreciate you." As she said the words she wondered if she was talking to Teresa or to herself. She shook her head slightly and focused back on what her friend was saying.

"That's so sweet of you. It hasn't been easy…" said Teresa.

"I know, I know. What'd you say the other day, though? Men, you can't live with them?"

They said together, "You can certainly live without 'em."

Teresa smiled. "Yeah, but life is more fun with them."

"Agreed."

Teresa carefully folded a shirt and put it back in a dresser. "So tell me more about what's going on at work and what you're learning from the person you've been talking to. What's her name?"

"PJ. She's terrific."

"It sounds like she's been giving you some great ideas. It made me start to think that maybe I could use some suggestions, too. I was seriously impressed with how you talked to Tom about not moving your desk. That was awesome. I know I would never have thought to do that."

El laughed. "Trust me. I wouldn't have either if I hadn't talked to PJ."

"That's just it. I can't talk to PJ, but I was hoping that you could give me some advice."

"Of course! I'd love to." El felt great that Teresa was asking for her help. She also felt a little panicked because she wasn't sure what to do. "Where do you want to start?"

"Well, you made me think about what's going on at work. As you know, my new boss, Mikaela, started just a few weeks ago. Since she came from outside the company, she doesn't really seem to know what she's doing so she hasn't really been giving me work the way that Kris had. She's giving more new work to some of the other team members, and it's really beginning to bother me."

El tried to imagine what PJ would say. "What do you think is going on?"

Teresa made a face. "I don't know. I've tried to be nice to her, but she seems to spend more time with some of the other people."

El pictured Carl. "What do you think they're doing that you're not?"

"Maybe she just likes them better."

"No," El assured her friend, "everyone likes you. I don't think that's it." She paused. "Let me tell you what PJ told me about getting what you want. You need to show the other person how you can help them to get what they want. And in order to do that you need to know what they want. What do you think are Mikaela's goals? What's she trying to do?"

Teresa shrugged. "I don't know. She hasn't given us her goals."

El tried to think of another way to look at it. "Let's look at it from her point of view. If you were her, what do you think you'd want to do?"

"I don't know. Maybe reduce costs, increase revenue. I'm not sure why the last manager was let go, but some of us think that it had something to do with not being able to control the budget. And actually, she did mention in a meeting that she was looking for ways to reduce vendor billing."

"Okay," said El. "What does that mean? How do you think you could help her with that?"

"She's looking for us to do some things internally that normally she would have to pay an outside company to do."

El threw up her hands. "Well that's perfect! How can you do that?"

Teresa shook her head. "It's really not that easy. There's no one internally that has the skills otherwise we'd already be doing it. And actually, it's something I've been kind of interested in but I'd have to get certified."

El stared at her friend. "So? Why don't you get certified?"

"You make it sound so easy. I'd have to take a six- to-nine-month certification program with an exam at the end. And it costs thousands of dollars."

"You were just telling us that you didn't have enough work to do.

What if you let Mikaela know that you want to support her idea of reducing the vendor costs by having you get certified? That way she could show her bosses that she has a plan to do it and you get certification. It all works!" she said triumphantly.

"But the cost," said Teresa. "If she's trying to cut costs, she's not going to want to spend money to pay for me to get certified."

"You don't know that until you ask. Stop imagining roadblocks that may not be there. After all, maybe the cost for the training comes out of a separate budget. Or maybe you can do a cost-benefit analysis showing that the cost of the certification would pay for itself within six months by reducing how much you need to use the vendors."

Teresa crossed her arms and looked skeptical.

El continued. "Has your company paid for other external training and certifications?"

"Sure, in other departments. Besides, if it would work, why hasn't someone else already come up with this?"

"Maybe we're the first ones to think about it this way. And maybe no one else is willing to put in the six to nine months necessary to get certified. But it sounds like you're interested in learning it."

"Well yeah. I think I'd be really good at it."

"And it would make you and your skills more valuable to your boss and company. And maybe this certification could open up some new possibilities for you in your company or outside."

"But I like my company. I don't want to leave."

"I know but sometimes things change and we need to be ready for them." El thought about the company she'd worked for right out of university and how much she loved it until it had been bought out by a bigger company and everything had changed.

El thought back to some of the things she'd learned. "You know what Jack said to me when I saw him tonight?"

Teresa smiled at the mention of Jack. "Okay what did he say? He's a man I'll listen to."

"Oh please," said El. "He told me that one of the most important things he's learned is to be open to new possibilities. You never know where the next amazing idea is going to come from." El tried to channel her inner PJ and said, "You can't just sit back and hope that people will hand you what you want. If you're really interested in this certification, let's find a way."

Teresa nodded. "Okay, good points. If I wanted to do it, what would be next?"

El and Teresa discussed some ideas. Teresa decided to research the certification right away to find out the specific costs and benefits. They developed a plan for what to say to Mikaela. First Teresa would talk about how she wanted to support the manager and her new goals and then she would introduce certification as a way to reduce the vendor costs.

El had Teresa practice saying it in a calm and positive way. "Remember, just think about it as a business project that can help the company. You need to take the personal feelings out of it. And if she doesn't agree to support the business project, it's okay. It's not about you. She'll still appreciate how you are trying to help her to meet her goals."

"Thanks El, you're the best," said Teresa as she signed off.

El worried about her friend the next morning. She hoped she hadn't changed her mind. Then she worried that she had given her friend terrible advice. What if it blew up? As the day passed, El continued to fret over Teresa.

Finally, late in the afternoon, she got a text from Teresa. "THANK YOU! Meeting went great. She loved it! She agreed to more than I asked for!!! Talk later!"

El read the text a few times. She got more than she asked for? She couldn't wait to hear what happened.

Teresa called a few minutes later and she oozed enthusiasm. "You won't believe it! It worked so well! I was really nervous and I almost chickened-out, but I knew you were going to ask me about it. So I did some deep breathing in the bathroom to calm myself down before I went in to see her.

"I talked about how I wanted to understand and support her and her goals just like we had discussed. She looked happy and mentioned the cost reduction so it made it a little easier for me to keep going. When I talked to her about the certification, she was really interested. When

I mentioned the time needed, she wasn't concerned at all because she said she was looking at long-term changes. Then I said the cost, and it didn't seem to bother her at all! I had found a few programs online and in person and I recommended the least expensive option, but she was way more interested in the most expensive one because she thought it had the best ROI. Can you believe it!"

"That's amazing!" said El. "You're amazing!"

"But that's not the best part," interrupted Teresa. "She thought it was such a good idea that she asked me to set up a task force to find one or two other people interested in going through the program with me, and we'd start a special project group focused on this area. I'm soooooo excited! And it's because of you, El."

"Oh no, no, no!" said El. "It's all you, Teresa. You came up with the idea. You did the research. And most important, you did it. You asked for what you wanted. And YOU got it! I'm so excited for you."

Teresa laughed. "I wouldn't have been able to do it without you. You're the best. Drinks are on me next week!"

"Now you're talking!"

"Okay, I'll talk to you later. I've got to tell my sister about this. She's not going to believe it! Thank you!"

El felt elated after the call. It was great to see her friend so happy.

She wondered, now what do I want to work on? And just as she wondered that, her phone rang. It was Eric Reyes from engineering.

"Hey, Eric. What's up?" El answered.

"Did you hear the news?" Eric's excitement was evident through the phone.

"What news?"

"Because you figured out why the Florida people were pissed off, and we were able to fix it, they've placed their biggest order yet. Their engineer called me and even asked if we could manufacture some devices to their specifications. Great work!"

El stared at her phone after they hung up. Something she had done clearly contributed to the bottom line. She was in shock.

Tom broke her out of her daze by requesting her presence in his office. For a second, she was worried, but then she reminded herself to keep an open mind and be like Jack. Whatever she was walking into would be a learning opportunity.

She knocked on Tom's open door and was shocked to see Carl and the other project managers crammed into Tom's office.

They burst into applause as she entered. El's eyes went from face to face and she felt her cheeks turning red. Had they heard already?

Tom said, "El, the CEO of Intermedstar sent Bob Worth an e-mail that specifically named you and Eric Reyes. They were ready to drop us as a vendor until you figured out what was going on. And now, we've increased sales this week by two percent already and have a whole new market open to us." El's mouth was agape. Was this really happening? Did they really send a message to Bob Worth, the CEO of her company?

Carl opened a bottle of bubbly and poured everyone a few fingers into plastic cups. The group raised their glasses, "To El," Carl said.

"To El" her colleagues cheered.

El took a sip of the champagne, and then said, "Thank you. I'm shocked. I got the idea of asking how we could help them be more efficient and effective from Carl, and I couldn't have found the solution without Eric. So it's really a team effort. To the team." She raised her glass.

They smiled and raised their glasses and drank, but no one else said, "To the team." One person said again, "To El."

The group started to disperse and Tom asked El to stay behind. When they were the only two left, he said, "That's the first time Bob has ever received an e-mail commending someone from our department. Nice work."

El couldn't help but grin. "Thank you."

"He instructed me to give you this," Tom said, and handed her an envelope.

She didn't want to open it in front of him so she just held it in her left hand and extended her right across the desk. "Thank you so much, Tom. For the surprise party, the champagne, and the chance to work on the Florida account." She shook his hand, though she really wanted to scream with joy and hug him.

She went to the restroom, made sure it was empty, and then locked herself into a stall. She let out a small squeal when she saw that enclosed in the envelope was a bonus check for $1000. Before she bottled up her excitement and faced the rest of the office again, she texted Teresa, Leticia, and PJ a three-sentence summary of the news. She also sent a bit longer text to her brother and to Derek.

Teresa, Leticia, and Jack responded immediately with "Congratulations! Let's celebrate." PJ said, "Congratulations. Let's set up a call to debrief." Derek responded, "Awesome! I just finished signing a 9-figure partnership and will be coming home in a few days so we can celebrate." El felt conflicted. While she was happy for him, did he really have to outshine her moment in the spotlight?

She texted back, "Nice!" and decided she'd rather celebrate her success with her support network, and bring them all together. She set up a group text to the girls, PJ, and Jack, "Are you available to celebrate on Sunday at 7 p.m.?" And she set up the debrief Skype with PJ for Saturday morning. El was sure PJ would suggest using this success as a segue into asking for the promotion and the raise, but El wanted to bask in the bonus and commendation afterglow a little more before plotting the next steps.

When El got home from work that evening, Mr. Fluffy was meowing at the door in greeting. She picked him up and twirled him around. "You know what? Our CEO now knows my name. He may not know what I look like or know me if we were on the same elevator. But he knows my name and he thinks I did a kick-ass job. Can you believe that?" Mr. Fluffy didn't look impressed. He looked queasy from the twirling and squirmed to be let down.

"Well you'd feel differently if you had to buy your own Blue Buffalo. That stuff is ex-pen-sive." She drew out the word while pouring a scoop into Mr. Fluffy's bowl. She ruffled the fur on his head and said, "But you're worth it." He ignored her as he inhaled the salmon kibble, licked the empty bowl, and then gazed up at her imploringly.

"You're too much," El said, and gave him another dozen nuggets, which disappeared instantly.

El went into her bedroom and removed her work clothes. She said aloud to the cat, "What should we wear?" Her two best friends both had dates, and Derek was still out of town. It was Friday night and she had nothing to do, though today had been one of the happiest days of her professional life. Maybe I should put this excess energy to good use and go to a fitness class, she thought. She opened her gym's phone app and checked out the course schedule. They were offering a spinning class, kickboxing, and a fast-paced flow yoga class set to reggae music. She changed into her tights and yoga-tank, ate a Kind bar and an apple, and filled her bottle with filtered water. She grabbed her yoga mat, phone, and keys; yelled good-bye and "I'll be in back in an hour" to Mr. Fluffy; and was out the door. Stretching and sweating to reggae seemed like a good addition to her day. And El figured she could get a smoothie and salad at the gym's café for an easy supper. She'd read and go to bed early. She wanted to be well-rested for her 8 a.m. Skype with PJ.

Chapter 10

As soon as PJ's face appeared on the screen, she waved at El. "Hi El, congrats! Loved getting your message! Tell me more." PJ was once again attired in yoga clothes: the straps of a hot pink and teal tank top were visible on the screen. She had somehow corralled her unruly curls to the top of her head with a hot pink scrunchy.

El, too, had opted for yoga wear. She grinned. It felt great to tell PJ the story about solving the customer problem. She ended with, "And the best part was the big bonus! It was so unexpected! It was awesome!"

"Sounds like you need to plan something fun to do with part of that bonus. Reward yourself."

That was just what El wanted to hear. She was going to use most of the money for bills but there were some cute earrings that she was thinking about getting. "I haven't really decided yet," she said, wondering what Derek would have to say about that.

PJ smiled. "I'm sure you'll think of something. You need to celebrate."

"That's why I'm hoping you'll join us on Sunday night. Just a few friends and my brother. I thought it would be fun."

"Thank you. That sounds great. I really appreciate it. I'm not sure I can make it, but I'll get back to you."

"Okay, please let me know."

"Now, tell me what's next," said PJ. "What are you going to ask for?"

El paused. "I want to ask for a raise and part of me thinks this is the perfect time, but in a way I feel a little bad about asking right now. I mean, they just gave me nice bonus."

PJ laughed loudly. "Seriously? El, that was a business decision based on the money they're making on this project and money they expect to make. That doesn't mean that you can't ask for a raise. This is the kind of thing that stops too many women from asking for raises. I hear so many different concerns. Some women are worried that it's a bad time for their boss. Or because they just took a vacation or because it's not a good time for the company. If I thought like that, there'd never be a right time."

El realized that she, too, had thought of plenty of those reasons.

PJ continued. "So forget all that. Actually, it's a great time to ask. Have you thought about what you want to say?"

This is what El was dreading. She wasn't sure what to say and didn't want to disappoint PJ. "I'm not really sure. Here's what I'm thinking about. I could say something like, Tom, I know it's not raise time but I'd like to ask…"

"Stop right there," commanded PJ.

"What?"

"Don't hand him an excuse. You're telling him why he should say no to you. Many women tend to use expressions like that to make the conversations go more smoothly, but they discount what you're trying to do. When you say things like, 'it's probably not a good time' or 'I know budgets are tight', it makes it easy for the other person to agree with you and say 'no' to your request. Instead, cut that part out. He knows it's not traditionally raise time; you don't need to tell him."

El nodded. "Okay. I'll just say, 'Tom, I'd like to ask you for a raise.'"

PJ smiled. "Much better."

El took a breath. "Then I'd explain all the research I'd done online with the salaries and talk about how my job has changed in the last few months, and how I'm now responsible for supporting more revenue growth. And maybe I'll talk about what some of the other teams have told me about how much they've appreciated my help and…"

PJ interrupted. "Have you already shared that information with him? Is this a reminder?"

"Well no, I hadn't shown it to him before. I felt like it was boasting if I passed on all the e-mails."

PJ stared at her.

El quickly added, "Of course I realize now that I need to let him know so I've started forwarding e-mails like that so he can see the effect we're having on the customer."

"The effect we're having on the customer?" questioned PJ.

El smiled. "I mean the effect I'm having. I'm still working on talking about what I've done without feeling like I'm bragging."

"Good," said PJ. "Let's get back to what you're going to say here. I think it's a great idea to have all of that information ready, but I would shorten it. One mistake I find women making in situations like this is talking too much because they're nervous. I find it's better to simply ask and then stop talking. See what Tom has to say. Then depending on his reaction, you can give him more of the information that's important to him." She smiled. "Use those great listening skills you used with your customer to hear what Tom is thinking so you can tailor your message. Sometimes I think women use the show up and throw up method. They keep talking hoping that their boss will agree with something.

"Instead, why don't you just say something like, Tom, I'd like to talk to you. I want to get a raise. I've been bringing value for the customers and the sales team that's made a big impact on our growth." She paused for dramatic effect. "And then stop talking."

"That's it?"

"Of course, there's more to it than that, but see what Tom's reaction is and what he has to say. Remember, keep in mind just what you did when you talked about the office move. Take as much emotion out of it as possible. Think of it as a business project."

El frowned. "That's not going to be easy."

"No, but it will be worth it. And when he replies, don't think that you need to answer right away. Take a moment to think about the best response. And if you get nervous, you can always thank him and say you'd like to think about it. Just remember to say it in a way that comes across as positive and professional not as nervous."

El smiled. "Yeah, I think I'm going to need to practice that one."

"Good idea, you can practice in the mirror, but I find it better to record yourself and play back how you look, or get a friend of yours to role play with you. Remember when we talked to Shayla about making positive mind movies?"

El pictured Shayla. "Yes."

"This would be a great time to practice. Picture you and Tom talking in his office and see yourself calmly asking. Then see Tom smiling and nodding and agreeing."

El's brow furrowed in worry. "But he might not agree."

"Yes, but you don't know that. Replace the negative mind movies you're playing in your head right now with some positive ones."

They talked for a few more minutes about what El could say, and she agreed that she would simply ask and then wait to see what Tom would say.

PJ paused. "How do you feel about doing it?"

El smiled. "Nervous, but good." Mr. Fluffy decided to join the call and El introduced him.

"Cute cat," PJ said before returning to the subject of asking for a raise. "Okay, let's talk about how to respond."

"What do you mean?"

"Asking is only part of the plan. You need to be ready to respond if Tom says 'yes', 'maybe', or the dreaded 'no'."

"Ugh."

"Yes, not a pleasant thought, but it's much easier to handle if you're ready. First, let's start with yes."

"That sounds like an easy one!" said El.

"It should be," agreed PJ. "But you'd be surprised to hear how often people mess this one up. The key is just to say 'thank you' and leave. The mistake some people make is that they're so excited they say something that doesn't help them. Don't say something like, 'wow, I didn't expect you'd actually say yes' or 'that's great, I was afraid you might not give it to me because of the way I'd messed something else up.'"

El laughed, but could totally see herself saying something like that if she weren't being trained better.

"I agree it's funny, but those are based on stories of what real people said because they were so excited. Of course, their responses made the managers wonder if they'd made a mistake. Don't let your excitement make you say something silly."

"Agreed," said El.

"Let's talk about what to say when you hear 'maybe'. Typically this is the most usual response since managers often can't make decisions by themselves. If they generally agree with what you have to say, it probably just means that they need to involve others or get approval from their manager or HR. Especially if you're asking for an off-cycle raise, they're going to need to do some work before saying yes to you. You can support them by asking what other information you could give them in order to help them to make the decision. If it seems like they're not convinced you deserve a raise, it might be a good idea to ask some more questions. Find out what they need in order to make the decision so you can get back to them with that information."

El jotted down some notes.

PJ continued. "And sometimes people just need time to process and think about it, especially the more analytical people. Recognize that and ask when would be a good time to meet again about this. Of course, you might also hear a maybe because the manager doesn't want to directly give you a 'no.' That will become clearer if they keep putting off a follow-up meeting. If that happens, you may have to ask what would need to change in order to get a raise. No matter what the reason is, it's important to thank your boss and let him know you appreciate the conversation.

"There's also another possibility. You may hear 'maybe' for a reason that has nothing to do with you. For example, maybe there's a reorg coming up or another big change and your boss wants to wait until after that happens. Remember, it's not all about you." PJ smiled.

"It's not?" joked El.

"I'm afraid not," said PJ. "And that's really important to remember if the answer is 'no.'"

"I really don't want to hear that."

"Nobody does, but the way you handle a 'no' can get you to a 'yes'. Let's put 'no' in perspective. Just because you get a 'no' doesn't mean that you won't get a raise, it just means 'no' for right now." PJ paused. "What do you think are some of the biggest reasons that managers say 'no?'"

"There's no money in the budget. The company isn't doing well." El thought about all the mixed messages her company gave saying that they were doing really well, but that they needed to be really careful about all spending because the competition was making things difficult.

"Yes, but remember there's always money for what the company thinks is important. What else?"

"The timing isn't right. You don't deserve it."

"Of all those, the biggest issue is if your boss thinks you're doing a bad job and you don't deserve it. This is where it's really important to use silence and ask good open-ended questions, and by that I mean questions that can't be answered by yes or no. Don't jump to conclusions. Don't assume that you know why your boss is saying 'no'. Find out.

"First take a moment to calm yourself and remember it's only business, it's not personal. Then go into problem-solving mode and get more information. You can ask, 'Can you help me to understand the problem?' Or you might say, 'Can you be more specific or give me some examples?' It's important that this comes across as curious instead of argumentative. You want to let your boss know that you really want to understand. You might also ask, 'What would need to change for me to get a raise?' That can help you to pinpoint if it's something you can work on or if it's something that's out of your control. Make sure to thank your manager for the information. Remember you want to view your manager as your ally. Most managers hate saying 'no' to their employees, so it's helpful to emphasize that you want to work together on this.

"And if you can't think of anything positive to say, it's better not to say anything. Just thank your manager and end the meeting. After you have time to process, you can go back and talk more."

PJ paused and El looked at her, thinking about how to put it into practice.

"Questions?"

El shook her head and laughed a little. "I don't know. The idea of hearing 'no' is so scary. It sounds better when you explain it."

PJ nodded. "It's not easy to hear 'no', but if you don't ask, you don't get. Look at a 'no' as a temporary setback. If you handle it well, it can help your manager to push to get you a raise in the future. I know lots of women are concerned that asking for a raise could upset their manager, but in my experience, if you handle it well, it can help build the relationship with your manager because they'll see your skills. I remember when a friend of mine went through this with her manager and afterwards he complimented her on her negotiation and business skills. So, are you ready?"

Mr. Fluffy jumped back next to El, and she scratched him under the chin. "Not really. But I will be. I want to write out some notes about how to respond. And I want to practice exactly what to say to Tom so I'll feel more comfortable asking him."

"When will you ask?"

"Do you think I should wait until after the meeting with the execs next week?

"Why wait? Tom just complimented your work and gave you the bonus. There's no time like the present."

El didn't feel ready, but she realized that she might never feel ready to ask. She took a deep breath and said, "Okay, I'll plan to ask on Monday."

PJ smiled. "Sounds good to me. Let me know how it goes. I'm sure you'll do great. Any other questions?"

El shook her head.

"Great. I'll get back to you about tomorrow night. Thanks again for the invite."

El waved at her. "Thanks for all the advice."

When the video ended, El turned to Mr. Fluffy and said, "Did you hear that? We have some work to do this weekend, but first I need to feel more centered." She unrolled her yoga mat on the living room floor, logged into YouTube and searched for a 10-minute guided meditation video for relaxation and focus. She knew she needed to calm the anxiety she felt even thinking about asking for a raise before she started making notes about what she needed to say. She sat on the mat cross-legged with her palms facing up on her knees. She said to Mr. Fluffy, "Please lay down and leave me alone for 10 minutes" and he actually seemed to oblige since he hopped onto the sofa and lay down. Then she pushed play on the video and let the soothing female voice and flute sounds transport her to peace.

Later, El made tea and toast, cut up an apple, and put some pieces of cheese on a plate and carried it to the table. She sat with a legal pad and her laptop and went through the e-mails from other teams and from customers that she had received complimenting her work. She created a folder for them and copied them to the cloud in case she ever needed them all in one place to support her raise request. She made notes on the legal pad of the things she already knew were important to Tom and how she was supporting those. Her mind was clear and ideas came to her rapidly. Instead of fear or trepidation, she started to get excited about the opportunity to ask for a raise.

As her hand and pen flew across the page recording her thoughts, El's phone lit up with a text. She looked at the screen. Her brother sent a link and said, "The teen that I hired was playing this last night so of course it made me think of you." El opened the link and heard The Cheetah Girls singing that they didn't want to be Cinderella waiting for a prince to save her.

She laughed aloud and texted, "I'm working on slaying my own dragons," and then added an appropriate meme. To herself and Mr. Fluffy she said, "And right now the pen is mightier than the sword," and smiled at her own joke.

"Want to borrow my buck knife?" Jack joked. For his ninth birthday he really, really wanted a knife, so their parents bought him one, but they would only let him use it when no other children were around, and he had to leave it on a bookshelf in the family's living room so their parents always knew where it was. Nine-year-old Jack whittled sticks for three days before he lost interest. El had no idea he still had that knife.

"Thanks. I'm good," she texted and added a smiley face.

"See you mañana," Jack texted.

El took another look at her notes and decided she had written enough for now. She flipped the page on the notebook and started a list of items she needed to get for tomorrow's party. Then she ripped that page off the pad, grabbed her reusable tote bags, wallet, keys, and phone and headed to the store.

Ninety minutes later when she had returned and was unpacking the groceries and putting the bottles of white wine in the fridge to chill, her phone rang.

"Hey, beautiful." Derek's voice sounded upbeat as usual.

"Hey. How are you?"

"Great, great. Things have gone so well here in Taiwan that the other partners want me to pop over to Hong Kong and then Singapore and meet with some other clients and potentials. I know I told you yesterday I'd be home in a few days, but that ain't gonna happen. Looks like another two weeks."

"Okay," El said.

"Don't be mad, baby." Derek said.

"I'm not," El said. "I'm glad things are going well for you." And she suddenly realized that she meant that, and that she didn't miss him after the first week or so. She didn't care about him being gone. On an intellectual level, she thought maybe she should feel guilty about that but she didn't.

"What are you up to?" Derek asked.

"Unpacking groceries. I'm hosting a party tomorrow to celebrate how well things are going for me at work."

"Oh fun," Derek said. "The girls?"

"Yes, and Jack and some others."

"Well, have a fun time," he said. "It's the middle of the night here, but I couldn't sleep so I thought I'd call. But I should really try again. Love you."

"Love you, too," she said, as he disconnected. She stared at the phone for a few minutes. Did she love him? Yes. But she wasn't sure she was still in love with him. It was nice of him to call when he couldn't sleep. Neither of them had been reaching out to the other very much. She remembered the times at the beginning of their relationship when they couldn't go to sleep or wake up without messaging or calling. Hearing his voice had given her a rush, and now she thought it was "nice". She missed the thrill of the new, of the can't get enough of each other phase. She wondered if she'd feel differently if they hadn't been apart for so long. At least the separation had given her plenty of time and space to focus on her career. She'd figure out what she wanted in her relationship once he returned. She trusted that when they were face to face, she'd know if she wanted to be with him or not.

For right now, she had frozen appetizers to put away before they thawed and a hungry cat to feed. Mr. Fluffy had come into the kitchen and with a very loud "meow" had taken her out of her head and into the present.

Chapter 11

Saturday afternoon, PJ texted to say she'd be at the party and she was bringing a plus one. El was instantly disappointed as she had been looking forward to introducing her to Jack. Then El texted Leticia and Teresa to see how their first dates went. Leticia texted back: Whooo, girl. Still on it. And El laughed aloud, sure her confident friend was having the time of her life.

Teresa called her in response, her video popping up on the screen. "What happened?" asked El when she answered.

"With what?" asked Teresa coyly.

"You know exactly what I mean!" shouted El.

Teresa laughed. "Oh you mean my date. It was good."

"Come on!"

"Okay, okay. It was amazing. It was great." She looked off to the side and said, "I don't remember the last time I had so much fun."

El was glad to see her friend look so happy. "What'd you do? Where'd you go? Tell me, tell me."

Teresa laughed again. "We started off with dinner. We were going to meet for dancing but I thought about what you said, you know, ask for what you want. And I wanted to talk to him a little more, not just go to a noisy club with him, so I suggested dinner and he recommended a cute little family-owned place he'd been to before. It wasn't fancy but the food was yummy. Best of all, it gave me a chance to hear more about him."

"And?"

Teresa's grin widened. "Jordan is sooo nice. He's the youngest of five boys and he helped put himself through school with scholarships and part-time jobs."

"Really?"

"Yeah, at one point he had three part-time jobs and didn't sleep much. He started out as a business major but decided he'd rather be a teacher. What a nice guy." She sighed happily.

"Did you go out dancing?"

"Yes, one of his friends recommended a club and we had a great time." She giggled. El couldn't remember the last time she had heard her friend giggle. Teresa talked more about the club and the evening.

"How about the goodnight kiss?" interrupted El.

Teresa grinned. "Do you think I'm the type to kiss and tell?" She paused as El made a face. "Okay, it was wonderful." She paused. "He walked me to my car and asked me for a kiss." She sighed again. "That was sooo sweet." She stopped as if she was savoring the moment again.

"When do you see him next?"

"Tonight." Teresa smiled. "When we were at dinner we started talking about movies and he asked me if I wanted to go see one so of course I said yes."

El was happy for her friend but felt a twinge of jealousy. It was another Saturday night that she would spend alone with Mr. Fluffy.

Teresa told El more about the high school that Jordan worked at and the dog he had adopted from a local shelter. The more Teresa talked, the more El thought he sounded really nice and a good match for her friend.

Finally Teresa asked El what she was doing and El told her about her talk with PJ.

"Are you really going to do it? Ask for a raise?" asked Teresa.

El grinned. "I promised PJ I would." She paused. "And I want to. I need to try." She immediately heard Yoda's voice in her head saying, "There is only do or do not, there is no try." She continued, "I mean, I deserve it and I'm going to ask for it."

Teresa frowned. "But it doesn't seem fair. Why should you have to ask? You do a great job. They should just give it to you."

El nodded. "Yeah that'd be great. But I can't expect other people to read my mind. I have to tell people what I want and be clear about it."

"It doesn't seem right. They should know you want a raise. It's obvious."

"You'd think so, but what's really obvious to you and me, may not be so obvious to others." El thought that was true outside of work, too.

Teresa continued to look unhappy. "Aren't you worried? What if Tom gets upset?"

"Yeah, I've thought about that. PJ says I shouldn't be so concerned about that. I shouldn't let it stop me."

"Uh huh," said Teresa, plainly not convinced.

"Okay," said El, "what do you think is the worst that could happen?"

"Well, he could get mad at you and that would make it really uncomfortable to work with him. I mean, I wouldn't want anyone angry with me, especially my boss."

"But would he really?" asked El, partly to Teresa and partly to herself. El had already thought about all the worst-case scenarios she could come up with. "Tom's a decent boss. I can't imagine he'd get really mad at me and make work uncomfortable, especially if I ask for it in a calm and reasonable way."

"But what if he did?"

El looked off to the side. "What if he was so impressed with me asking for a raise that he said yes right away?" She laughed. "And what if he was so happy when he heard my negotiation skills that he promoted me on the spot? And what if they gave me a company car and a huge entertainment budget? What if all those things happened instead?"

Teresa shook her head. "You're not really going to ask for a company car and an entertainment budget, are you?"

"No, of course not. But why do we always assume the worst?" She told Teresa what Shayla had told her about replacing her negative mind movies with positive ones. "And I think this can work with guys, too," said El, laughing.

"I'd be happy to make some positive mind movies about Jordan," agreed Teresa.

"You know what else PJ told me? She told me I should ask myself what would a successful guy do. And I thought about it. I bet the guys I work with don't waste time worrying that Tom is going to be mad at them if they ask for something that they deserve. They see it as business not personal. And I need to start doing the same thing. And I need to stop hinting about what I want and hoping that the other person is going to read my mind. If I want something, I'm going to ask for it. She's right,

I just assume that the company is going to give me money just because I work hard, but in reality nobody's going to just hand me money or a promotion."

"But what if the answer is no?" asked Teresa.

"Then I guess I'll have to learn how to deal with it. But what if the answer is yes? Wouldn't that be awesome? After all, if you hadn't asked Jordan out, you would not have had that great night out, nor the second date tonight."

Teresa nodded. "Good point. You guys pushed me to do it, and I was afraid he'd say no but then I thought getting a yes outweighed a possible no."

"That's just what I'm thinking, too. Getting a yes to a raise outweighs how uncomfortable I am about asking."

"Good for you!"

"PJ also gave me some ideas about what to say after asking. Can I go through a few with you?"

"Absolutely."

El talked through some of the different responses with Teresa. El had been a little nervous about how she would handle it if Tom said no, but Teresa's comments made her feel more confident. She thanked Teresa for her time and input and said she'd see her at the party.

After the call, she looked at her messages. She saw one from someone she had worked with more than five years ago. She hadn't heard from him since then, but he was contacting her to see if she knew of any available jobs. She opened LinkedIn and sent a message letting him know she couldn't think of any, but would send him any leads she found.

Still feeling great from the phone call, she decided to click on possible job matches. She was surprised to find two listings that looked interesting. She briefly felt bad about even looking at them. It felt disloyal. "It's only business, it's not personal," she said aloud to herself. She argued with herself that she didn't want a new job. She liked what she did so it didn't make sense to apply. Then she remembered how she felt when she lost her job after her company was purchased and decided that it wouldn't hurt to see what was out there.

She found an old copy of her resume and realized that she hadn't updated it since she had started her current job. She frowned. She knew she should keep it up-to-date so she spent part of the afternoon adding her current job and highlighting the Florida project win and the new U.K. project. She made the same updates to her LinkedIn profile. And then she thought, what the hell, and drafted a cover letter and then hit submit on the applications.

The party had been underway for 20 minutes when El's front door opened and PJ stuck her head in. Her curls provided a multi-dimensional black frame for her almond eyes and high cheekbones. She wore an emerald green silk tank over fitted jeans and emerald strappy heels. Jack, who was standing next to El, said, "Wow," at the sight of PJ.

PJ's surprise plus one trailed her through the doorway and caused El to grin and yell, "Shayla!" Shayla's red glasses and ruby lips were the only bit of color in her otherwise black ensemble: sheer blouse, jeans, short boots. She hugged El and said, "So nice to meet you in person, and I hear congratulations are in order."

Never one to be shy, Jack inserted himself into the group of women and said, "I'm Jack, Rella's brother and resident bartender." He shook their hands. PJ grinned at Jack and said, "Cinderella and Jack. Wow. How did you two ever survive childhood?"

Jack laughed. "It was torture until I was old enough to understand and make euphemistic beanstalk retorts." He wiggled his eyebrows at her dramatically, which caused El to roll her eyes and everyone else to laugh.

"I'd ask what PJ stands for, but please wait to respond. Your hands are empty so I need to first fetch you and Shayla drinks. What would you like?"

Jack led them towards the food on the kitchen counter and he poured their Chardonnays. When everyone had drinks in hand, Jack turned down the light jazz music and said, "To Rella. The best, and my only, sister. Congratulations on your bonus. Thank you for spending it partly on us. And may you continue to kick ass in the office and in life."

"Here, here," El's friends all echoed with their glasses raised. El thought the moment couldn't get any better as she felt so much love in the room. Even Mr. Fluffy took that moment to let out a loud "meow" that may have been in support (though it could have been because Teresa shooed him away from a piece of chicken). El thanked each one of them for being a part of her journey and said she couldn't have or would not have wanted to do it without them, before turning up the music and grazing on the assorted appetizers, alongside Shayla. El told her about the presentation she needed to give to the senior management and Shayla gave her some pointers about how to appear super confident and poised. Then she launched into a story about a recent conference she keynoted in Copenhagen.

Over Shayla's shoulder El could see her brother and PJ resume their banter, both smiling and laughing often. Leticia popped into the kitchen to pour herself another glass of pinot noir. "The bartender is busy," she joked.

"So I see," said El.

Shayla turned to see where El and Leticia were looking, and she laughed aloud. "It never fails," she said. "PJ is a man magnet. Every straight man that catches sight of her wants to be near her and to make her laugh. And I don't blame them. We've been together for almost five years and I still think she's the most stunning person in any room."

El worked hard not to show her shock. It never even occurred to her that PJ and Shayla might be a couple. "She is," she said, "and I hope she lets Jack down easy. For all of his bravado, he has a fragile ego."

Leticia said, "Jack is one of a kind." Then she turned to Shayla. "How'd you meet?" Shayla told them about the conference in Atlanta where she was a speaker and PJ was in the audience and approached her afterwards, asking for public speaking pointers, and how they had ended up discussing it over coffee, which led to drinks and then to dinner. They had found they had similar tastes in music, loved Thai food more than any other kind, and both loathed Terrence Malick's "Tree of Life." "People have bonded over less," Shayla joked.

"True," Leticia said. "I had a 30-hour date this weekend that revolved around mutual physical and sexual attraction and not much else." She laughed.

"Well sometimes that's what one needs," Shayla said.

"Exactly," Leticia said, and she lifted her glass in a toast. "To having needs met, short-term, long-term, personal or business."

"I'll drink to that," El said, and the three of them clinked their wine glasses together.

At that moment, El's phone vibrated on the counter showing Derek calling over FaceTime. "Nice timing," Leticia said, looking at El's phone.

"Should I get it?"

In response, Leticia picked it up and answered. "Yo, Derek. You're missing the party."

"Hey, Leticia. I'm in Asia."

"We know. How long you there for?"

"Don't know. Looks like it may be a few months now."

"Does El know?"

A hush fell over the party as Leticia handed the phone to El. "Hey, beautiful," Derek said, "Sorry to miss the party."

El forced herself to smile. Why was he calling now? she wondered. She had told him when she was having people over.

"Say hi to everyone, Derek." She rotated the phone so he could see them wave at him. Then she turned it back to see him and stepped into the other room.

"Sorry, hon. I forgot the party was tonight but I wanted to say hi."

"Hi. What'd you say to Leticia? Does El know what?" She immediately felt bad that it came out so harshly. She quickly adjusted and said, "Is everything okay?"

"Yeah, yeah, better than ever. It looks like they might need me a little longer. It's not going to be two more weeks. It's going to be months."

El was silent.

"I promise, babe, I'll be back as soon as I can. And we can get away on our own little vacation. Please don't be upset. Business is going great. They need me here."

"I'm not upset. I'm really, really surprised. This started out as a short trip." She heard her voice get louder and she took a breath. "It's fine. You need to be there. I'll be just fine." She forced another smile. "See I've got my friends here. We're celebrating. I'll be fine. You take care of your business."

Derek looked relieved. "That's great, beautiful. Yeah, I'm sorry for interrupting your party but say hi to everyone. You deserve it. I'm going to go so you can get back to the gang. I love you."

"Love you too," repeated El before the call finished.

She looked at the phone and shook her head as if trying to clear her mind. She took a deep breath and said, "Yes, I do deserve it. I definitely deserve it."

Talk stopped when she walked back into the living room. She smiled and said, "What?"

"A few months?" asked Leticia. "Are you okay?"

She waved her hand dismissively. "No big deal. We'll work it out later. Come on, this is a celebration." She looked at her brother. "Bartender, I think we need some refills over here," she said nodding at some empty glasses.

Jack eyed her briefly and said, "Coming right up! Who needs a fresh drink?"

Teresa brought out a plate of hot bruschetta with figs and a cashew-based cheese, and another of red pepper and goat cheese. People gathered around and started talking again. The group grazed on other delicacies that Jack had brought, including the stuffed poblano peppers he had added to the menu. He delighted in explaining how he made them and his future plans for the trucks.

"I hope you have enough room for a little dessert," El said. She had gone to her favorite bakery and got a variety of butter cookies, macaroons, and mini cannoli.

"I don't have room for dessert," said Leticia. "Is that from Aldo's bakery?" she said, when she saw the tray of goodies. "Okay, maybe I have a little room." She laughed as she reached for a macaroon.

Most of the guests decided they also wanted to try the macaroons and cannoli. The conversation briefly changed to "mmmms" as they sampled the sweets.

"I'm not the only one who's had a win this week," El announced to the group. "Teresa did a great job asking for something this week and got it."

PJ turned to Teresa and said, "That's great. Let's hear it."

Teresa looked embarrassed. "It's not a big deal…"

PJ interrupted her, "El thinks it's a big deal. Don't start minimizing your good work. You need to celebrate what you do."

"Here, here," said Leticia raising her glass to her friend. "There are plenty of other people ready to dismiss us and what we do. We need to own our success."

"Okay, okay," said Teresa. "You're right. But I don't like feeling like I'm boasting. It wasn't a big deal."

"Teresa…" warned PJ.

"I'll tell you. Actually, El gave me the coaching."

PJ laughed and said, "Please own it first, then mention El. Women don't take enough credit for what they do. I want to hear what you actually did. But first, stand up straight, shoulders back, feet apart, chin up, smile."

Teresa followed the directions.

PJ continued, "Now, I want to hear you say it with confidence. What would a successful man say? How would he own it?"

Shayla turned away laughing. It looked like she was used to this. And Jack blurted, "He'd be shouting it from the rooftops," and then he laughed.

Teresa took a breath and told the story about how she had asked her boss to pay for her certification. PJ interrupted her several times to remind her to say it with more confidence. When Teresa announced that her boss had approved the more expensive certification and named her to head a new task force, PJ and the group applauded. "Now, that's owning it," said PJ. "How does that feel?"

"Great. Just great!"

"And even if you'd gotten a no, you should still feel great about it because you asked. A no doesn't mean no forever. And like I always say, if you don't ask, you don't get. Right, El?" PJ said.

El laughed. "So true!"

Teresa said, "Now I'm going to thank El." She looked at PJ as if to challenge her to try and stop her. She told the group how El had coached her and challenged her to talk to her boss.

"I couldn't have done it without PJ's help," said El.

"Ugh, you're not going to get all mushy now, are you?" joked Jack. The group laughed as El gave her brother the stink eye. She talked about how PJ's coaching changed how she acted at work and what it meant to her.

PJ said, "I talk to plenty of people but not everyone is willing to do something about their situations. You agreed that if we met, you'd take action and share it. And you did. I know it's not easy. I couldn't be prouder."

Soon after, PJ announced that they were going to have to leave. "After all, El, you have a big week ahead." They left with hugs all around and the rest of the guests left soon after. Jack offered to stay and help clean up but there was little left to do since Leticia and Teresa had tidied up throughout the evening. El gave him a big hug as he left and locked the door after him.

El sat down on the sofa and smiled. "It's you and me, Mr. Fluffy," she said, as he came over for some attention. The party had been a success and she felt great about it. "PJ was right," she said, as she scratched him under the chin. "I've got to get ready to talk to Tom. Time for bed, buddy."

She was looking forward to the next day.

Chapter 12

When El awoke early the next morning, she reviewed the notes she had made and practiced what to say aloud as she did her hair. She put on her best bra and panties under her favorite navy suit. She knew she was the only one who would know she was wearing them, but they gave her extra confidence. She was still feeling the positive energy from the night before and planned to ask Tom for a raise that morning. She got to work early, found time on his calendar, and sent him an invitation. As she planned for the other meetings she had that day, she saw a personal e-mail notification from a name she didn't recognize but from a company she did. It was one of the companies she had submitted her resume to. The recruiter wanted to set up a phone meeting to talk about the position.

She felt a wave of self-doubt. She wasn't even sure she wanted the position. What had she been thinking? She liked her job. She didn't want to waste the recruiter's time if she wasn't definitely interested in the job. She also felt disloyal. After all she was going to ask Tom for a raise, how could she even think about applying for another job?

Then she stopped and thought about what PJ would tell her. What would a successful guy do? She smiled and decided it was only business, not personal. The recruiter had suggested several potential times for a phone meeting and she picked one for the next day.

After she hit send, she realized she liked the potential of another company being interested in her, even if she really didn't think she wanted the job.

El's nervousness mounted as the morning progressed. She tried to keep focused but it wasn't easy. She was glad her meeting with Tom was at 10:30 so she didn't have to wait all day.

Twenty minutes before the meeting, she went into a conference room and reviewed the notes again. She replayed the positive mind movie in her head several times, seeing herself looking calm and Tom smiling and agreeing. Part of her brain told her it was nonsense and it would never happen that way, but she tried to push those doubting thoughts aside. Feeling silly, she stood in a power pose for two minutes with her hands on her hips like Wonder Woman as she had learned from the Amy Cuddy Ted Talk video. She took a few deep cleansing breaths and she decided she was as ready as she was going to be.

She smiled as she walked into Tom's office. She sat down and asked about his weekend and heard about his son's soccer team's win.

Then Tom said, "What's up, El? I can't imagine that you're just here to find out about the final score in Flynn's game."

This was the moment for which she had prepared.

"There is something else, Tom. I've been thinking about what we discussed last week and I want to talk to you about getting a raise now. I've been bringing value for the customers and the sales team that's made a big impact on our growth." El stopped and resisted the urge to keep talking.

Tom frowned. El was fine with that because she had expected it. She continued to smile and feel confident.

"But El, I thought we discussed that last week. It's not raise time yet. We can talk about it in a few months."

El nodded. "I realize that it's not the typical time of the year, but I understand that raises and promotions can happen at different times when there is a reason." She thought briefly about the surprise bonus she had gotten the previous week.

It was almost as if Tom had read her mind. "Yes, but El, you just got a good bonus last week."

El was prepared for that also, and so she calmly said, "Yes, Tom, thank you. I really appreciated getting the bonus for the work I did with Intermedstar. It meant a lot to me to be recognized for my work. And I know that work helped to save a customer, get a large order, and generate other potential orders." She mentioned the potential revenue generation that the sales team had calculated and then she paused.

"I believe the work I've done with that project, the U.K. project, and the successful roll out of the promotion prototype shows that my work is getting results for our team and across divisions that connects back to the bottom line." She then mentioned specifics of some other high impact projects.

Tom nodded as she spoke, but he still frowned.

After she talked about her work, she stopped. She resisted the urge to be nice to him and let off the hook by telling him it would be okay if now wasn't a good time for a raise. Not talking wasn't easy. She continued to smile calmly while her head felt like it was exploding.

"Hmmm. I'm going to need some time to think about it," he said.

El was ready for this. "Thank you, Tom, I appreciate you thinking about it. How can I help you? What information would be useful for you to know or for other people to know? In case you need to let HR know, what would they need?" El remembered PJ's comments about working with your manager and helping them to solve the problem together.

Tom's frown lessened and he rubbed his chin. "Hmmm, let me think about that."

"I can get you any of the numbers from the last projects and show how they positively impacted sales if it would be helpful." She suggested a few key metrics and offered to e-mail the information.

"I'm not sure."

El waited; she didn't want to jump in too quickly. She was starting to feel more tense She had been hoping for a more positive reaction. She reminded herself it wasn't personal, it was only business. She tried to focus on this as a project. He's just questioning the project, she said to herself. It's just a project.

Tom finally said, "I'm going to have to talk to Marc and HR to see if it's even something we can do." He shook his head. "I just don't know. Budgets have been tight."

"I understand; it seems like budgets are always tight. But I also know that our group is really making a difference and my work has helped sales meet and exceed some of their targets." She mentioned a few things that other groups had told her about her work and how it helped them. She offered to forward e-mails from key people.

Tom still wasn't smiling, but he had stopped frowning. "I can't make any promises. I'll just see what I can do."

"Thank you, Tom, for going to Marc and HR to see what can be done. It means a lot to me. I appreciate all you've done to help support the direction of the projects and my career."

"You're welcome. I do appreciate all you do for the team. I just don't know."

"Let me know how I can help."

"Okay, will do. Anything else?"

"That's all I wanted to talk about regarding the raise. I also wanted to check in with you regarding the presentation tomorrow. I sent the slide I'm going to be using and wanted to see if you had any other comments."

They spoke for a few minutes about the presentation. Tom liked the slide and didn't have any suggestions.

Right before El left his office, she thanked Tom again for his support of the projects and his willingness to talk to Marc and HR about her raise.

She walked to a nearby empty conference room where she closed the door and let out a deep breath. She sat quietly for a minute and said to herself, I did it. I really did it. Wow.

Her mind started racing about what she did wrong. She shook her head and commanded herself to stop. I'm going to enjoy this and not dissect it, she thought.

She texted short messages to Leticia, Teresa, and PJ letting them all know she had done it. And gotten a maybe. It felt great.

She sent a separate e-mail to PJ letting her know about the interview she had scheduled for the next day and asked for some suggestions about how to handle the salary question at an interview.

She soon got an e-mail back from PJ with quick suggestions:

"If the recruiter asks you about salary, they want to know if you fit into their range. You can lose leverage if you give the first number. Do this:

1. Say: I need to know more about the position to be able to answer that. Can you tell me more about…?

2. If they ask again, ask them what is the range for this position? Sometimes they'll tell you.

3. If they really want to know, say here's the range I've found from

my research of similar positions and that's what I'm looking for.

Go get 'em!"

She thanked PJ and reviewed the salary research she had prepared for her meeting with Tom. She felt ready for the interview. Now she just had to get through the presentation to the senior leaders.

Hours later, right after El returned home from the office, her buzzer sounded. A deliveryman stood at the door with a package marked global express. She signed for it and brought it into the kitchen so she could use a knife to open it. Mr. Fluffy jumped on the counter to investigate. He sniffed the box.

El cut through the tape and slid the distinctive orange box with the brown ribbon from the package. The card from Hermes Hong Kong had Derek's scrawl:

Congratulations, beautiful. I love you. -D

She moved the box out of Mr. Fluffy's reach. Then she undid the ribbon and opened the orange lid. Inside the tissue paper was an enormous pale yellow silk scarf bearing "Panthera Pardus" and the image of a golden-brown and black leopard and green tufts of grass. Her breath caught at the exquisiteness of the details, the weight and softness of the silk. She was sure it had cost him a fortune. She picked up her phone and called. He answered on the first ring.

"Oh my God! I love it! Thank you so much," El squealed.

"You got my gift."

"Of course. It's beautiful, Derek."

"I know how much you like cats."

El laughed. "True."

"I know we've been apart for a long time and that this extension of my time here has been a big surprise to both of us. I feel bad about it, but the companies we're working with are asking if I can relocate here for maybe six months to a year now. And my partners think it might be good, both for the clients we just acquired and so I can get to know others and expand the business further." He paused.

El was rubbing the scarf against her face, and it took a few seconds for her ears and brain to register what he said. When it did, she stopped and sank onto a chair. "So you'd be moving there?"

"Temporarily, yes. It's one hell of an opportunity and I've made so much progress already."

"I see," El said. "I'm happy for you, Derek." And she was. He had always wanted to be a mover and shaker on the worldwide stage of finance. He made no apologies for his ambition. She realized she could learn from him regarding that.

"So I need to tell my partners later today my decision. And El, I was thinking, maybe you should join me. I'm getting invites to all kinds of social functions. It's part of the job and culture here to be seen at the right functions and events. I could use a beautiful date. Want to move with me?"

El was stunned. What about her job? What about her life in California? She couldn't just put it on hold for him. She *wouldn't* put it on hold for him, to be his arm candy. WTF? "Derek, I love the scarf, and I appreciate your offer. Being in a foreign country with you might be fun. But I have a life here, and a job, and I may be getting a promotion and raise soon. I even have a different company who wants to talk to me about working for them. I've worked hard. I can't walk away from that."

"But beautiful, you wouldn't have to work hard. You could volunteer here. I could get you on a charitable committee or something. I make enough for both of us."

"Derek, I love my work. And what about Mr. Fluffy? I can't abandon him. And I won't abandon my team and the projects I'm leading. I'm—" She started to say she was sorry but realized she wasn't and she shouldn't say it so she stopped herself.

"I'm sorry you feel that way, El. I thought we could have a grand adventure. If you change your mind, let me know soon. Right now I have to go back into a meeting." He sounded annoyed and maybe a little sad; it was difficult for El to tell from his voice.

"Thank you again for the beautiful scarf, Derek. Let's talk again soon."

He disconnected without saying he loved her or anything else in response to her suggestion of talking soon.

She then did something she rarely did and initiated a three-way call between herself, Teresa, and Leticia and told them about receiving the scarf and the whole phone call. When she was done, Leticia said, "He has some cojones thinking you'd give up your life to help him further his career and social standing."

Teresa said, "I don't know. I think it is kind of sweet and romantic that he wants El to be with him."

"Ick. She'd be window dressing. Women have come too far in life and their careers to do nothing but make their men look better," Leticia said.

"But he loves her," Teresa said. "He could get anyone to escort him. Instead he wants El to move with him and live with him. He even said he'd financially support them."

"I love my job. I love working," El chimed in.

"Well I do, too," Teresa said. "Some days. But on others it would be nice to have someone else pay the bills and shoulder the stress and decision-making."

Leticia said, "We didn't go through all of that schooling to become kept-women. And we've fought too hard as women to become anything we've wanted and to get equal pay. His offer is insulting."

"It doesn't have to be," Teresa said.

El cut in. "I'm not exactly insulted, but I also don't feel like he understands what I want or how I feel. And since he hasn't been here during all of the work I've done to advance myself, I can't expect him to understand or to know. That's why I need to have a long talk with him. I appreciate you guys listening to me and for providing your input and support. I love you both."

"Any time, El," Leticia and Teresa said in unison, and Leticia added, "Just don't do this, okay?"

"I'm not going to," El said. "And the next thing for me and Derek to decide is what his relocation means to our relationship. But I'll worry about that a different day. Right now I need dinner, a walk around the block for some semi-fresh air, and a good night's sleep. I have a meeting with execs tomorrow. It's a career first and I need to do well."

El played more songs from the Girl Power play list as she showered and got ready for work the next morning. She watched a couple of videos on ways to tie Hermes scarves and found one particular way to wrap the fifty-five-inch square scarf around her neck and to knot it as expertly as a Parisian. It elevated her sale-find blazer and pants to a previous unreached level. She felt more sophisticated than she usually did, and she smiled at her reflection in the bathroom mirror. Mr. Fluffy sat on the counter. "Wish me luck," she said to him, before she hurried out the door.

The meeting was in a conference room on the executive floor, which was four elevator stops above El's (though she took the stairs to get in more pedometer steps). As she entered the room, she saw Tom in a gray suit and Marc in a navy suit and their next level boss plus two other men El knew only from the photos of the company's executives that were on the website. Three other men El did not know at all, and only one other woman was present besides her.

"El," Marc said as she took the first steps towards the table. He reached out and shook her hand. "Congratulations. It's not every day Bob gets an e-mail extolling our employee's virtues. Well done."

El's face broke into an uncontrollable grin at the compliment. "Thank you," she said.

Tom smiled at her. "You ready?"

"Absolutely," El said.

Marc motioned for her to sit between him and Tom, and one of the managers El didn't know called the meeting to order. He thanked them for their time, and then said that before they got on with the rest of their agenda, he wanted to make sure they all knew about the rare positive e-mail Bob got from a customer. El was taken aback. She had no idea it was such a big deal and that everyone was talking about it. But she also realized that she made the right decision regarding relocating. Now was her time. She needed to seize the moment. She thanked the meeting facilitator for the accolades, and then launched into the information on the slide and asked her questions.

Almost everyone in the room seemed eager to share with her their expectations regarding the U.K. project. Only the woman remained quieter than the rest and sat a bit back from the table. At one point, Tom glanced at his phone and then shot off a message to someone.

El jotted notes and took down three action items for her team to follow up on immediately. She thanked them for their time, and then excused herself from the rest of the meeting, just like Tom had instructed her to do when he had told her he'd try to get her on the agenda. The rest of the meeting was above her pay and position grade, and that was fine with her.

But as she was leaving the room, Tom trailed behind her, and shut the conference door so they couldn't be overheard. She was surprised he had left the meeting. "Nice job, El."

"Thank you."

"Hey, I just got a message. There's an issue with a big customer in New York and sales is actually asking for your assistance. They want to leave this afternoon to get there in time for a meeting in the morning. I forwarded you the e-mail."

"Uh, okay. I can do that," El said, her mind creating a mental checklist of what she'd need to do to make that a reality.

"Thank you," Tom said. "I'm sure you'll take care of it." He turned and went back into the conference room.

El opened the e-mail on her phone. Sales sent their flight info to El, plus a brief dossier on the customer. It was a quick trip in and out with the outbound flight at 4:30 p.m. Since she'd be back late the next day, she didn't need anyone to check on Mr. Fluffy.

As El went down the staircase to her floor, she felt a bit like she was Tigger bouncing with joy. She knew what she and the team and the U.K. project needed. Higher ups knew who she was and that she was doing exceptional work. Sales was eager to have her intervene with a customer again. She felt appreciated and valued. She was sure that raise was in her near-future.

In the meantime, she had a few things to do including typing up her notes and calling a meeting with the U.K. team for Friday, reading the dossier, and preparing for the interview with the recruiter. El decided since she needed to pack for the trip, she would leave the office before lunch to have time to get ready and then talk to the recruiter from there before heading to the airport.

Before she left, she sent a note to all the executives with a copy of her slide. Several of them had asked about the metrics so she had offered to send it to them.

She finished packing just before she called the recruiter from Proponics. It was the first interview that she could remember where she didn't feel nervous. She wasn't sure if it was because her mind was on the New York trip or because she was thinking about the raise she was expecting to get. In any case, she was able to easily sound confident and comfortably answered all the questions. She highlighted her recent accomplishments without feeling stressed. I guess this is what happens when you don't care so much, she thought.

The job sounded interesting and she asked a few questions about why the job was open and the biggest pain points of the department and company. Then the interviewer said, "We want to make sure we're in the right range and are not wasting your time. Please let me know what salary you're looking for."

El was glad she had checked with PJ. In the past, this question had made her stumble. She said, "Thank you for checking. I'm really interested in hearing more about the job so I can understand the level and responsibilities."

"I can understand that, and I'll be happy to do so, but we want to make sure that we're in the ballpark with your salary needs." The recruiter had moved to PJ's Step 2 and El was ready.

"Absolutely, I want to make sure that our needs match. Can you let me know what's the range you're looking at for this position?"

The recruiter paused, and El wondered if she was going to get the information or not.

"We'd like to hear what you're looking for," responded the recruiter.

Step 3. El said, "Here's the range I've found for similar positions." She named a wide range that she had found in her research from several websites. "Does that match the range you're looking at?"

"The range is similar."

"Great. It looks like we're in sync so I'm interested in hearing more about how my skills could be used here."

The recruiter told her more about the job and answered all her questions. He said he would get back to her within the next two weeks. She thanked him and left for the airport shortly after.

She checked her e-mail as soon as she reached New York to see if there were any messages from the sales team. She was surprised to see a message from the Proponics recruiter asking for her to meet with the hiring manager the next day. She quickly responded that she couldn't because she was on a business trip but would be happy to meet with them on Thursday.

Kate, one of the executives in the meeting, had responded to El's message and slide. Kate had some additional questions that she had not asked in the meeting. El sent a message answering what she could and asked some clarifying questions to learn more about what Kate was looking for.

She met with the sales team early the next morning for breakfast. They filled her in on the situation with the customer and the part that they wanted her to play.

When they got to the customer's office, the meeting did not start out well. Just as the sales team had explained, the customer was angry and spent the first ten minutes ranting.

Instead of defending her company and the products, El did her best to hear and understand what the customer had to say. She let their manager talk and repeated back the key messages she heard. She knew that her colleagues wanted to jump in and explain their reasons but she had asked them in advance to let her listen uninterrupted to the problems.

As the customer continued to vent, she could hear his volume start to reduce. His angry tone slowly changed. She continued to listen and focus on really understanding his concerns and issues. After he felt heard, the mood of the meeting changed. He still wasn't happy, but he was willing to discuss some possibilities.

After the meeting, the sales team took El out for coffee and thanked her for her help. Nick laughed and said that was probably the best meeting they'd had with that customer. He was never happy. El promised to look into some of the issues that the customer had brought up and would get back to them.

On the plane home, she thought about how she would tell Tom about this and how it would help her with her raise request. She also thought about Derek and what it would be like to have him gone for six months to a year. She sighed. She didn't want to dwell on that.

Back at the office the next day, she worked with another team on issues the New York customer had raised. Even though they hadn't come up with a solution like the one for the Florida company, they had formulated some answers. She put the information in an e-mail to Tom to let him know how she had helped the sales team.

She was glad to get home at the end of the day. The hiring manager from Proponics had suggested a meeting with her after work so she made herself a quick salad and ate while she scanned the headlines. She dialed into the meeting and met the hiring manager, Parveen, who talked to her about the job. As she described the team and their upcoming projects, El thought that it could be interesting if she didn't already like her current job so much. Parveen ended the interview letting El know how much she had enjoyed the meeting and that they would get back in touch soon.

El let out a deep breath after she signed off and decided she needed some quiet time. She changed out of her business attire and into colorful leggings and a t-shirt. She unrolled her yoga mat and spent the next 30 minutes stretching. Mr. Fluffy tried to join her but quickly got bored when she wouldn't pet him. She tried to calm all the thoughts in her head that were swirling about Proponics, her job, and Derek.

She had been trying her best to not think about Derek but it wasn't working. She alternated between being angry at him for even suggesting that she should just take off and leave everything she had, to being happy that he wanted her to be with him, to worried that they wouldn't be able to make it work. At that moment she was berating herself for not appreciating his offer more. It showed how much he cared. She told herself she shouldn't focus so much on him wanting her to leave everything.

The yoga helped relax her and so did half a glass of wine as she binge-watched episodes of a favorite show. She finally dragged herself to bed.

On Friday, work was relatively quiet as she pushed to get responses for the executives and answers for the New York project. She was intently focused on an e-mail so she didn't notice someone come into her cubicle until he spoke. "Hi El, how are you doing?" asked Carl, making her jump slightly.

She laughed, "Great, Carl. Sorry. I guess I didn't see you."

"You look pretty intense," he agreed. "I wanted to stop by and congratulate you. I heard that your presentation for the executives went very well."

She almost discounted her work and said it was nothing, but then she thought of PJ and said, "Thank you, I appreciate that. I worked hard on it and was really pleased with how it turned out. It showed me how interested they are in the U.K. project and helped me to think about how to move things forward."

"Good for you." He paused. "You had mentioned that you might be able to help my team. Would you be available to meet about that next week?"

"Absolutely. I'd be happy to see what I can do."

"Terrific, I'll check your calendar and set something up."

They chatted a few more minutes before Carl left and El went back to her work. She had a lot to do next week but she felt like she was positively moving forward with everything.

Chapter 13

Late Friday afternoon Tom called El into his office. As she walked in, Tom said, "Why don't you shut the door?"

Hmmm, she thought, maybe this is the answer to my raise question already. She closed the door and noticed Tom did not look happy.

He played with a pen on his desk as he said, "El, I want to talk to you about your raise request." He paused. "I talked to Marc and HR and it was not approved."

El stared at him, trying to take it in. She willed herself to keep a neutral expression. He was saying no. He was really saying no to her.

She wasn't prepared for this and frantically thought back to what PJ had said. What do you do if the answer is no? It's only business, she said to herself. Remember, no means no for right now. How could she handle this in a positive way?

Tom was talking again. "El, it's not that you're not doing a terrific job. You're doing great. It's just that it's not raise time and there's no reason to give a raise now out of cycle." He paused to see her reaction.

She took a breath and said, "Hmmm."

He jumped in. "El, you know if it was just up to me, I'd give you a raise. It just doesn't follow company policy."

Talk about it like it's a project, she said to herself. Work with your boss. "Thank you, Tom, for talking to me about it. I do appreciate you going to Marc and HR."

Tom looked a little relieved.

El continued, "I just want to make sure I'm clear. The issue is that it's out of the raise cycle. Is that it?"

"Yes, yes, that's the problem."

"And you support my request, right? You think that my work

deserves it?"

"Yes, and there's no disagreement about your work. Marc is very happy with it."

She wanted to whine. What about the executive presentation? What about the U.K. project? What about Intermedstar? What about New York? It wasn't fair! She knew that saying these things would make her feel satisfied for a moment but wouldn't get her a raise.

Instead she said, "So help me to understand, what do I need to do to get a raise?"

"You will get a raise. When it's raise time."

She felt stuck and decided to try something else. "What can I do to get the highest raise possible when it's raise time?"

"Just keep doing what you're doing," said Tom.

"Yes, but I don't just want an average raise, I want to get a high raise that takes into account all the value I'm bringing. How can I do that? I'd like to meet with you to make sure I'm on track for that. I want to know if there's anything else I need to do."

"Uh okay, we can meet again and talk about it."

"Okay, I'll set up something on your calendar."

"I am sorry that I couldn't have given you a better answer today. I do think you're doing a great job."

El thought, I'm sorry too but said aloud, "Thank you. I appreciate your support, Tom, and I'll look forward to our meeting and working together on this." She got up on shaky legs and left the office.

She quickly walked to the ladies room and sat in one of the stalls. She needed some privacy and couldn't risk someone coming into a conference room where she was sitting. She closed her eyes and did some deep breathing. She couldn't believe that Tom had said no. Sure, PJ had prepared her for that possibility but after the week she had, she was sure the answer would be yes. She shook her head. What a crummy way to end the week.

She went back to her desk, trying in vain to focus and ended up leaving a little early. When she got home, she considered texting her friends to let them know what had happened, but she suddenly felt too tired. Mr. Fluffy seemed to notice and came over to rub against her leg without meowing his annoyance that she hadn't fed him yet. She leaned down to scratch him. "You'll still love me even if I didn't get a raise, won't you?" He purred and she took that as a yes. She fed him and turned on some relaxing jazz. She heated up a frozen meal and barely tasted it as she thought over and over about the meeting and what it meant.

The next morning she let herself sleep late, but then checked the schedule and headed out for an exercise class right before lunch. She wasn't hungry but had a protein shake for lunch and then texted Teresa and Leticia about the meeting with Tom.

Leticia came right back with "No WAY! Is he crazy? That is sooo wrong!"

Teresa texted, "Oh no! Let me know if you need to talk."

El smiled. She appreciated both of her friends and knew that they would support her. She was deciding whether she wanted to talk to Teresa or not when she got a text from Derek, asking "can U talk now?"

She took a breath. She wasn't sure if she wanted to talk to him now but maybe it would be nice to let him know what had happened with the raise. She texted him back and his picture popped up on her screen.

"Hi, beautiful," Derek said.

"Hi, handsome."

"I've been thinking about you and I wanted to talk."

She smiled. "That's so sweet. I wore the gorgeous scarf you gave me to the executive presentation and thought of you." She paused. "But I have to tell you about the awful meeting that I had with Tom yesterday." She started to tell him and as soon as she said that Tom had said she would not get a raise, he interrupted.

"That's it then. You can leave and come here. They don't appreciate you."

"But…" El wanted to tell him how she had handled it.

"What's the but? Did he change his mind? Did you get the raise?"

"No."

"Okay, then it's settled. Here's what I'm thinking. You can put your furniture in storage, I'll pay for it. And you can check into early termination of your lease. Mr. Fluffy can stay with your brother." And with that, Derek compressed her whole life into a few problems that could be easily taken care of.

"But…I don't know."

Derek stopped smiling. "I thought you wanted to be with me."

"I did. I do. But I wasn't expecting it to be like this. You didn't ask me to move in with you. You didn't propose. You just said, hey, I need someone to go to social events with me so leave your life and move here. I'm not some business accessory, Derek." El slammed her mouth shut. She watched him grimace. She didn't know where those words came from. She hadn't planned to say them. Then again, that was how she felt.

"Why are you making this so difficult?"

"Difficult? Because giving up life as I now know it…and Mr. Fluffy… is not an easy decision, nor should it be. I have responsibilities, Derek, and a job I love, and people who rely on me. And other than yesterday's raise setback, I've liked the way my life has been heading the last couple of months. I'm finally being recognized for my accomplishments and it feels good." El tried to maintain eye contact with Derek but the anger and hurt in his eyes hurt her. She did care about him, but she wanted more from him than what he was offering. She deserved more.

"So you'd give up the chance to be with me, to explore Asia and society here, on the off chance you might get a raise and more recognition in the future?" He shook his head. "You're betting on the wrong hand. I'm holding all of the aces."

El didn't gamble but she was pretty sure she knew what beat the aces, so she said, "Derek, I'm not betting on a hand. I'm betting on myself, and I'm a royal flush."

"Hmmph," he muttered. "I'd bet a million bucks that you'll still be in your shitty apartment and struggling to make ends meet a year from now. Most women would jump at the opportunity I gave you."

His last two sentences pissed El off, and she finally exploded, "One, I am not most women, and until a few seconds ago I considered myself your girlfriend. Two, I've made a helluva lot of progress in many areas of my life during the last few weeks but you'd know nothing about that because you haven't been here and have barely even talked to me. And when you have, it's mostly been to brag about your accomplishments. I'm happy for you, Derek; you're living your dream. That's great for you. But guess what, I'm finally living my dream, too, and I now know that my dream does not include being with someone who treats me like you do. Good-bye, Derek." Before he could respond, she disconnected from FaceTime.

El tossed the phone on the couch cushions next to her, and she started to shake from the adrenaline coursing through her. Fat tears rolled down her cheeks. Mr. Fluffy curled onto her lap and gazed up at her as if to say, "I'm sorry." She ran her hand through his fur and tried to find comfort in it, but she felt so emotionally raw.

She had no doubts about what she had just done. On some level, she knew that it had been coming. What pained her was how someone she had once loved and who claimed to love her could believe in her and her abilities so little. Did he really think she could best serve him and the rest of humanity by being his arm candy and some society hostess?

It sounded like he was willing to offer her the "opportunity" to act as his accessory. It felt like he was treating their relationship like business when it should have been personal.

Sure, she saw value in being on boards and doing charitable work. And she wanted to do those things some day, but in a Marissa Mayer kind of a way, working her way up the corporate ladder and being recognized for her transferable business skills, not for being the partner of some wealthy and powerful male.

Her tears had stopped. She stretched her arms up over her head, careful not to disturb the napping cat too much. She reached for her phone and group texted Teresa and Leticia: "Dumped Derek."

Leticia responded with "Bringing wine. Be right over."

Teresa texted, "Stopping for pints of Halo Top but on my way."

El grinned and her heart warmed. Her best friends really were the best. She gently pushed Mr. Fluffy from her lap, stood, wiped off the cat fur stuck to her leggings, and walked into the bathroom to see if her mascara had created raccoon eyes while she cried.

After a day and a half of too much wine and ice cream, binge-watching a TV series, and alternating between anger, sadness, and relief, El was ready to plunge herself back into work projects. She could barely believe that just a week ago on Sunday night, she and her friends were celebrating. She sighed.

On Monday morning, she made it to the office by 7:30 a.m. so she could call the U.K. client before their day ended. She had decided to focus her energy into making her projects succeed whether they gave her a raise or not.

Tom stopped by her desk and seemed to make a special effort to be friendly and asked about her weekend. She smiled pleasantly and said it was fine. She focused on being professional and on not showing any emotion. Tom sounded uncertain at her response and went back to his office.

The recruiter from Proponics sent her a request for an in-person interview at their office and she quickly accepted. She sent an e-mail to Tom letting him know that she'd need to leave a little early on Friday afternoon. Normally, she'd feel bad about taking some time off but she didn't feel bad about interviewing elsewhere any more.

She sent a message to PJ about how well the interviewing process was going and asked if she or Isabel could talk with her about salary negotiation for a new job. She felt good about the way she had handled it at the first meeting with the recruiter and wanted to make sure she was prepared for the next interview. After all, if her current company didn't value her contributions, maybe it was time to move to some place that did.

PJ quickly sent back a message and suggested that she contact Isabel. El had Isabel's phone number and e-mail from when she had sent a message thanking her after her last session. She sent Isabel a text asking if they could have a call.

That afternoon, El met with Carl and his team. She carefully listened to their issues and agreed to join them later in the week for a brainstorming session. As they left the meeting, Carl said, "El, how are you doing?"

El smiled. "Just fine, Carl."

"You seem a little quiet today."

"I was just really trying to listen to what your team has to say."

"Okay, thanks. I really appreciate it and I think your questions were spot on. It gave the group a lot to think about. You bring some very useful perspectives. I think it can really help us to jump-start this thing."

"Thanks." El smiled and said, "You have a great team."

Weirdly, Tom made a point to say good-bye to her at the end of the day by stopping as he passed her cubicle. El replied in a pleasant but neutral manner. She didn't want to show how upset she was, but, at the same time, she didn't want him to think that everything was going well.

El scheduled things each night so she didn't have time to think about Derek. Monday night was exercise at the gym, Tuesday she worked late on a proposal since Teresa started her class and Leticia was preparing for court, on Wednesday she scheduled time with Isabel, and the reggae yoga class was on Thursday night. She and the girls had agreed to meet for happy hour on Friday after El's interview so she could debrief with them over a well-earned drink and dinner.

On Wednesday evening after El had changed out of her work clothes and finished a supper of chicken salad and iced tea, Isabel's picture came up on the computer and El saw her familiar brown pixie cut hair and friendly smile. El quickly thanked her for taking the time to talk to her and said how much she appreciated the HR perspective. Isabel waved her hand and said it was no trouble. She said that she had heard from PJ how well El was doing and she was happy to help. El brought her up to speed on the Proponics job and her questions about how to handle the salary negotiation. She described how she had used PJ's suggestions.

Isabel asked her some questions about the situation. She wanted to know if the recruiter was internal or external. El said internal and then asked why that mattered. Isabel explained that external recruiters only got paid if you got hired. They might appear to be on your side and push to give them salary information so they can help you, but ultimately you have to remember that they work for themselves, not you.

"I recommend that you avoid telling your current salary. It's not going to help. More and more states are changing the rules so companies can't ask about current salary. Many recruiters won't ask and if they do, you should make the conversation about your salary expectations."

"Why are the rules changing?" El asked.

"This makes it more fair for job hunters. Companies don't need to know what you made at your last job in order to make you a salary offer. That can hurt women who might be making less than their male counterparts. By focusing on what a job is actually worth, we might begin to get closer to salary parity between men and women."

"Hmmm," said El. "I never thought about it like that."

"Here's what I suggest if they offer you the job and give you a salary number. Take a breath and pause. Repeat the amount and pause again. Wait to see what they say next. Sometimes they'll tell you more information such as potential for bonuses or a salary review opportunity in six months but remember none of those are guaranteed.

"No matter what the offer is, don't accept it right away. Thank them. Tell them how excited you are about the job and say you'll need to think about it and get back to them. If, in the rare instance, the salary is more than you expect, great. Go home and celebrate and then call them back the next day and accept. Though I still think that you should ask for more anyway. That way they won't think their offer is too high. Really though, in most cases, the salary will be good but not amazing and you should ask for more. What's the worst that will happen?"

"What if they don't like that I've asked for more and they take back the job offer?"

Isabel laughed and said, "Then it's good you find out early that they're not the right people to work with. In my entire career, I've only heard of that happening one time and the applicant found out later that there were a lot of problems at the company. She was glad she hadn't accepted the first offer and gone to work for them."

Before El said anything, Isabel continued, "What does PJ say? 'What would a successful guy do?' Studies show that most men will ask for and get a higher salary when offered a new job. A majority of women are happy to get the job and accept the offered salary, so they lose out on additional pay. Let me point out that this is way different from negotiating to buy something like a car. In that negotiation, you're never going to deal with those people again so you're just focused on the price. In this negotiation, these are people you're going to work with so you want to pay attention to the relationship also."

El frowned. "But how do you do that?"

Isabel shook her head. "Don't worry. It just means that you act in a professional and positive way so they continue to see you as someone they want to work with. When they offer you the job, thank them and talk about how excited you are to become part of the team and how much you're looking forward to working with them and helping them meet their goals. Then when you ask them if they can do any better on the salary, they'll want to see how they can make it happen. They'll need to go back and check with someone else, so you want them on your side. Remember, if you've gotten to this point, they want to have you take the job. This is the most leverage you're going to have. You need to use it."

"What should I say? And you're right about women. I've never negotiated a starting salary ever. I've just taken what's been offered. I've never even thought about negotiating." El frowned at her own ignorance.

"Don't talk too much. After you thank them and talk about how excited you are, you can simply say, 'I'm curious about the salary. Is there any flexibility?' Then pause and see what they say. If you need to, you can add more information that supports the higher salary from either salary data or the value you are bringing."

"That sounds great. Okay. What about if the salary is way too low? I talked with the recruiter about a salary range but the bottom of that range is too low for me to consider it quite frankly."

Isabel laughed. "That sometimes happens. You want to continue to be professional and build a relationship with the recruiter and hiring manager. Sometimes it's a new position and they don't realize that they really need a more senior level person. You may have to give them some more information to think about based on your experience so they can consider if they need to upgrade the description and the pay. Or maybe they made a mistake and thought you were a lower level. Make it clear what you're looking for and maybe there is another, higher position that will become available that could use your skills. Let them know that you're happy to consider other positions or maybe that you can recommend others for positions at that company. Good recruiters are always looking to expand their networks. Which reminds me, we haven't yet connected on LinkedIn so I'll send you an invitation."

El smiled. "Thank you. That would be great." She realized that she needed to start expanding her online network so she added that to her To-Do List.

They spoke for a few more minutes, and El thanked Isabel again for all her help.

At the end of the call, El turned to the cat. "Well Mr. Fluffy, wish me luck on Friday." She went into her closet and looked at her clothes, pulling things out and trying them on to determine what she thought made the best interview outfit. When she thought she had it all pulled together, she FaceTimed Leticia.

"Yes?" Leticia looked smashing as always in a tailored black power suit, jacket nipped in at the waist ever so slightly and a raspberry silk blouse adding the splash of color. She grinned at El.

"Does this look appropriate for my interview on Friday?"

"Put the phone upright on your table and step back. Let me see it all."

El did as instructed and hammed it up with a hand on her hip and a slow spin.

"Nice. Now let me see you strut?" Leticia joked.

El sashayed like a super model towards the phone and back while both of them laughed. "Don't hate me, honey," Leticia's voice stopped El mid-stride. She grabbed the phone and brought it to her face.

"I could never…."

"I love what you're wearing, but it is a little bland. I really think the Hermes would boost it. It's a power scarf, and you want to show you're a professional and a woman to be reckoned with. It'll channel your inner French woman." Leticia smiled.

"Just call me an auburn Audrey Tautou." El laughed. "But more seriously, I just read she's worth like $20 million. I'd take it. The French scarf it is." She removed it from its orange box, wrapped it a few times around her neck, and knotted the two ends together. And then she looked in the mirror, while holding the phone so Leticia could see, too.

"A little lipstick and you're good to go," Leticia said. "And if the recruiter is a heterosexual male, you may steal his heart like the prince at the ball."

"Funny," El said, grinning. "I'm not out to steal hearts. Just a big fat salary and an incredible opportunity at a company where I'm appreciated."

"I hear you, sister. And speaking of companies, I need to get this brief finished before tomorrow, so back to work for me. Thank you for allowing me to be your stylist. We've created another winning work look. Love you." Leticia signed off as El said, "Love you, too."

"Well, Mr. Fluffy. At least we have that settled. Please try to keep the cat hair to a minimum. Ha." She put the whole outfit on one hanger in the closet, with the scarf looped over the top.

Then El turned on the Girl Power playlist and shook her butt around the bathroom to Donna Summer's "She Works Hard for the Money" as she removed her makeup, washed her face, and got ready for bed.

Chapter 14

On Thursday, she met with her team on the U.K. project for most of the morning and they made excellent progress. Everyone on the team had his or her assignments and everyone was moving forward, and so far the client was happy. That afternoon, El met with Carl and his team again where they brainstormed all over the Dry Erase boards in the conference room. El took photos of what they wrote with her phone's camera, as she wanted to be able to look at them later. She knew that one of Carl's team members had recorded everything on her computer, but sometimes it helped El to see the chaos of the brainstorm; it triggered her creativity and helped her come up with solutions. One thing that she sensed during their brainstorming was how deep in the weeds Carl's team was; El thought they had maybe lost sight of the big picture. She made a mental note to talk to Carl about the 30,000-foot view once she had some time alone with him.

That evening, after sweating to reggae yoga, El spent two hours researching Proponics to make sure she understood what they did. She looked on GlassDoor to get a sense of their salaries and what employees past and present thought of the company. She read company press releases and news coverage on them. She read open job hiring notices. She made notes and she wrote down questions as they came to her. Then she spent time reading over the notes and organizing them into a cohesive flow, and she chose half a dozen questions that could be asked. She put those on a notecard that would fit into her jacket pocket.

On Friday morning, El ate a big healthy breakfast, as she wanted to start the day off right. She put a prepackaged salad and some crackers in a bag for lunch because she didn't want to take time off for that since she was leaving work an hour early. Then she dressed in the outfit she and

Leticia had put together for the interview. She would head to Proponics straight from the office. She applied her makeup extra carefully while blasting "Confident" by Demi Lovato.

Shortly after she got to the office and started drinking her coffee while answering e-mails, Tom appeared in her cubicle. "El," he said.

"Yes?" She turned her chair to face him.

"I just wanted you to know that a couple of the execs have told me during the last week how much they appreciated you taking the time to find out their expectations for the U.K. project. Sometimes people rush so quickly into projects that they may not think to confirm what the leaders are really looking for. So, thanks." He smiled.

El returned the smile. "My pleasure, Tom. Thank you."

"Well, keep up the good work." He left her cubicle.

"Grrrr," she mumbled when she was sure he was out of earshot. So the execs appreciated her and her work but still wouldn't give her a raise. That pissed her off. She took a deep breath to a count of five, held it for five, and exhaled for seven, like she did in yoga class. She did it two more times. She knew it was one way to release anger, frustration, and sadness. At the end of the three cycles of mindful breathing, she was a little less angry and hurt, but just a little. And she was a lot more grateful for the interest Proponics was showing in her. She took a few moments and closed her eyes and envisioned a positive mind movie, where answers to the interview questions came easily to her, where she and the interviewers seemed in sync, and where it ended with them inviting her to join their team at a huge salary increase and the possibility of a healthy bonus. El smiled and opened her eyes.

Carl was standing in the doorway of her cubicle smiling back at her. He was wearing an evergreen suit, a lilac shirt, and a royal purple and green plaid tie. On anyone else El was sure it would look stupid, but he rocked it, with shiny black loafers. "Whatever you were thinking made you look radiant. You look so happy."

El laughed. "Thank you." Inside, she felt a little silly but shrugged that off. "How are you this morning, Carl? Please sit down." She motioned to the empty chair.

He set his coffee mug on her desk. "My team appreciated having someone new guide the brainstorming. Thank you."

"You're welcome. It was my pleasure. And I've been thinking, Carl. I believe one of the reasons the team is having problems is because they are so caught up in every minute detail of the project, including stuff that is usually handled by business ops and not our teams, that they are losing the scope and breadth of what they are supposed to deliver. I think it has made them stuck."

Carl's eyes widened and El wondered if she had gone too far.

"That's brilliant!" Carl exclaimed. "Of course that's the problem. I have been too close to it, too, to see it. This, this is exactly why I wanted you to work with us. Bless you." He grabbed his mug off her desk and almost ran from her cubicle. El laughed at his retreating back and his excitement.

Just then El's phone buzzed. A text from Jack said, "Yo, Rella. Mom keeps texting about you and D. She's worried about you. I've told her while you aren't doing the happy dance, you haven't slit your wrists either. Call her."

El shook her head. Sometimes her mom was a bit much. She took her phone, laptop, and legal pad with her to a conference room. Before she started on more work, she called her mother for five minutes to let her know she was, indeed, fine, but very busy with work so she'd call her again tomorrow to talk more in-depth. She signed off with, "I know you're sad about me and Derek but in many ways he was more toad than prince. I love you."

El spent the rest of the day running from what seemed like meeting to meeting. Fifteen minutes before she needed to leave, she went into the bathroom and brushed her teeth and her hair, straightened out her clothing, reapplied her lipstick, and took one last reappraising look in the mirror.

One of the women in Carl's group emerged from one of the stalls. She complimented El on the scarf and on how sharp she looked. El smiled. "Thank you," she said.

"And thank you for all your help yesterday," the woman said. "Whatever you said to Carl this morning made such as difference. We refocused our efforts and reread our original mandate, and just a few minutes ago, the answer to our biggest problem appeared right in front of us. Weird. It had probably been there all along. We were just too close to everything to see it. It was like you brought us a miracle."

The woman looked like she was about to hug El, so El took a step backwards and said, "That's so great! I'm happy for your team." Then she looked down at her watch and said, "Oh no, I'm running late. See you later," and left the restroom for the elevator. Proponics awaited her arrival.

El got there early and sat in her car for a few minutes reviewing her key points again. Then she took a few deep breaths and went in. She was scheduled to meet with the hiring manager again, several team members, and a senior manager. El was quickly brought into a conference room and offered some water.

Parveen joined her a few minutes later. El recognized her from their initial meeting. She was shorter than El had expected and her long dark hair was in a loose bun. Parveen welcomed her warmly and let her know that she'd be back at the end of the interviews to take her on a tour of the office.

The interviews went well and El felt all of the people she met would be good to work with. She was worried though that this company was smaller than her current company and not as advanced, so she'd have to build some of the processes that she was used to. In a way, it almost felt like stepping back a year. She shrugged to herself. It was a new industry and new opportunity; she should focus on the positives.

At the end of the interviews Parveen showed El where their group sat. She proudly pointed out the cafeteria with free sodas and coffee and deeply discounted meals and mentioned some of the other company perks, like discount gym memberships and work from home days. Parveen shook El's hand and said they would be in touch soon.

El drove to meet her friends. She got to the restaurant a few minutes early and checked her messages. Leticia was running late. She had said not to wait, so when Teresa arrived, they ordered. As they munched on chips and guacamole made at the table, El talked about the interview and her impressions of the company. When she paused, Teresa asked her, "How much do you really want to work for this company?"

"The people are nice and I could really work with the products. I think it would be good."

"Yes, but would you like it more than your current place?" El started to interrupt and Teresa raised her hand signaling her to stop. "It sounds okay, but I'm not hearing a lot of enthusiasm. If you're going to get a new job, I want you to get it for the right reasons. I want you to be going toward a great new job." She shook her head. "I don't want you running away from your job because you didn't get a raise yet. I don't mean to butt in; I just want what's best for you."

El smiled at Teresa. "I know you do. I want it to be the right thing, too. I just wish I could have gotten the raise. I really like what I do, but I'm pissed at Tom right now. The executives are happy about what I'm doing, but they're not willing to pay me more. I just don't understand it." She sighed. "Let's see what happens. They may not even offer me the job."

"That's ridiculous! They'd be idiots."

They both laughed. Leticia joined them soon after and demanded an update on the interviews. Both friends also wanted to hear how El was feeling and if she'd heard from Derek at all. (She hadn't.) They drank a toast to the future. They agreed to end the night early. Teresa suggested a movie the next night and Leticia wanted to go shopping on Sunday and asked El to come along to help her pick out clothes. El knew Leticia never needed any help in choosing clothes as she was always the best dressed of the three best friends. El suspected that her friends wanted to keep her busy, but she wanted a little alone time. She promised to text them if she wanted to get out of the house or if she wanted them to come over.

El had a quiet weekend planned. Her brother called and so did her mother. She told both of them that she was fine and just needed some relaxation time. She cranked up the Girl Power playlist while she reorganized her kitchen cabinets and drawers. Mr. Fluffy originally sat the on the counter supervising, but eventually he either couldn't stand all of the commotion or grew bored. He moved to a sunny spot on the living room floor and took a nap until El was finished.

On Monday morning, El was surprised to see a meeting invitation with Kate on her schedule for 10:30. Kate had additional questions about the project. El quickly accepted it and sent a message asking if Tom needed to join. Kate's administrative assistant let her know that

Tom had been notified but didn't need to attend.

Tom again stopped by to say hello and ask about a small matter about which he could have easily e-mailed. She wondered if he was concerned that she would leave. He should have thought of that before telling me that I wouldn't be getting a raise, she thought.

At 10:15, El went up the stairs to the executive area and waited outside of Kate's office. Her assistant told El when to go in. El was surprised to see how large the office was. Behind Kate's desk were floor to ceiling windows, making it very bright.

Kate stepped from behind the massive desk to greet El. She was tall and thin with a simple turquoise dress that El bet cost more than most of her wardrobe. As she extended her hand, El noticed her many bracelets and large rings. Kate gestured to the couch and chair near the desk and they sat down.

El had prepared herself for the meeting by asking herself what would PJ say. So when Kate started the meeting by complimenting her on the presentation, El thanked her instead of saying what she would have normally said, "It was nothing." She could hear PJ telling her to take credit for what she did.

Kate asked for more details and El provided her with the information. At the end of twenty-five minutes, the executive smiled and thanked her and let her know she'd be in contact if she needed anything else. El quickly left, happy to get away from the quiet executive floor. She wondered if she would be able to get used to more meetings with the executives. That was one part of her new projects that she hadn't expected. It was exciting and terrifying at the same time.

At the end of the day, Gregor, the Proponics recruiter, e-mailed El and they set up a time for a call early the following day. When she arrived at work the next morning, she found a conference room and called him. They chatted for a few minutes, and he talked about the positive feedback he had gotten from everyone who had interviewed her.

"I have great news, El. We think you're the right person for the team, and we'd like to offer you the position."

"That is wonderful! I'm so excited to hear that. I really liked meeting everyone. They seemed like a great team. And the projects sound very exciting, something I can really jump right into and where I think I can really make a difference. I also think the office space is great. I can see it's a place where you can really get things done."

"Thank you, El. We really like it."

Gregor then offered a starting salary that was barely more than what El was making and some stock options that would pay off if the company ever went public. El thought about what Isabel had told her. She paused and repeated the salary amount and waited.

Gregor quickly jumped in. "Yes, and we think the options are a real differentiator. You'll also be eligible for a review after the first ninety days."

She took a breath. "Thank you. I have a question."

"Sure, El, what?"

"The salary." She paused. "Is there some flexibility with the salary?"

"Well, that's the offer."

"I want to let you know I'm very excited about the opportunity and I think I can make a real difference. I know that the salary ranges I've seen were much higher than that and considering my background and experience, I had expected it would be on the higher side."

There was silence, and El worried that she had gone too far and had upset Gregor.

"Well, I really don't know. That's the salary that's listed for the job." He paused, and El resisted the urge to jump in and tell him not to worry about it.

"I'll tell you what," he said. "I can let them know that you asked and I'll get back to you and tell you what they say."

It was better than a no but El felt butterflies in her stomach. She thanked him and they chatted for a few more minutes.

She got off the phone and wondered if she had just messed everything up. She took a few deep breaths and decided she was fine. Actually, she was more than fine. She had done it. It was uncomfortable but she had done it. And whether she got the job or not, she had made the effort.

El texted PJ, Isabel, Teresa, and Leticia: "Got an offer. Negotiating more money."

"Good for you" was the individual response from all four of them. Leticia added a "you go, girl" to the end of her text. El's heart felt happy from the support.

El spent the rest of the morning in her cubicle working on her various projects. Right before lunch Carl and Tom walked by her space and Carl said, "Knock, knock." He and Tom were both in navy suits with white shirts and yellow ties.

El laughed. "Come in. Did you intentionally dress like twins?" She joked.

The men looked from one to another as if they were noticing the similarities for the first time. Carl blurted, "Next time I'll text you so we don't do this again." And then he chuckled.

Tom grinned and said, "El, Carl and I were debating between getting something at Starbucks downstairs or running next door to the Chinese place. We thought you might join us."

Instantly, El was a bit suspicious, as she had never been invited to lunch by either of them before. She hesitated in replying, so Carl filled the void with, "We could use some fresh air."

With that, El agreed. "I could use some time away from these office lights." She smiled, stood up, and grabbed her purse. She didn't relish another salad from Starbucks since she ate them often, so she said, "My vote is for Chinese."

Carl did a quick bow and said, "What the lady wants, the lady gets," which caused Tom to laugh and El to wish everything in life was that easy. "Thank you," she said, and stopped herself from adding "but if Tom would rather…" PJ was in her head reminding her to ask for what she wanted and then to STOP TALKING.

At lunch, over beef with broccoli, cashew chicken, and vegetable chow mein and rice served family style, Tom talked about his kids' weekend soccer games, and he mentioned in passing how much he grew to appreciate his wife over the weekend since she was away tending to her ill mother and he had to manage the kids' schedules himself.

Carl laughed and said, "That is why I think dogs are so much easier. Their schedules are so routine, and their demands are feed me, feed me, pet me, pet me. Speaking of which, how's your cat, El?"

"You have a cat?" Tom asked. "What kind?"

"Oh a big fluffy one," Carl answered for her.

"It's true," El said. "Mr. Fluffy is his name. And he's maybe a six on a 10-point demanding pet scale." She pulled out her phone and showed Tom Mr. Fluffy's latest photo. El had no idea how Mr. Fluffy exuded an attitude of bored tolerance in every photo, but somehow that's what always came across.

Tom said, "Wow. That's a lot of fur. My kids really want a dog, but I know my wife would be the only one taking it out and walking it and feeding it. We tried goldfish, but of course they died. And then we tried hamsters, but I couldn't even get the kids to take care of those and of course them being nocturnal didn't help."

El thought back to PJ's hamster analogies. She smiled. "Hamsters are cute, but you're right in that any animal is a responsibility and sometimes kids aren't ready for that kind of constant work."

They ate in silence for maybe a minute, when Carl suddenly switched to work topics saying he had heard a rumor that Marc was up for a promotion and was being moved to oversee a new kind of product for the company. Tom nodded his head once. Carl chewed thoughtfully and then asked, "Are you in line for Marc's job, Tom? You'd be a great director."

El was wide-eyed at the two of them. She marveled at Carl's easy rapport with Tom and wondered how he knew about Marc's promotion, as it had not been announced formally. But, she thought, he always seemed to be on top of information.

Tom said, "I am one of the eligible candidates, yes. But we'll see what happens. So many people and positions are in transition as we ramp up two new products and finalize our purchase of Xraytronics." El forgot the company was buying one of its suppliers. It had no direct bearing on her job nor on the division she worked for so she hadn't paid that much attention to the purchase announcement. But now her brain felt like it was processing at computer speed and she could hear PJ, Isabel, and Leticia's voices in her head telling her how much all of it mattered, as it all affected the company's bottom line and everyone's advancement opportunities, including hers. El made a mental note telling herself to maintain focus on the broader picture.

Carl nodded his head and said, "It's such an exciting time in our industry. I'm grateful we all work together."

"Me too," El said, before her brain caught up to the words leaving her mouth. "I've learned a lot from both of you." She raised her teacup in a toast. "To us. We're awesome." She laughed at her confidence.

"Here, here," Carl said. And the three of them clinked their cups together.

"Yes, lots of transitions," Tom said with a far-off look in his eyes. Then he looked them in the eyes and said, "Both of you have been doing excellent work and have really made a difference in our teams. Thank you."

When the check came, Tom picked it up, saying it wasn't like he got to take them to lunch every day.

"Thank you, Tom, for lunch, and to both of you for getting me out of the office," El said. "I had fun." And she realized that she had. She liked working with them. She liked talking to them. It wasn't as scary as she once believed. And, if I must leave them for a new job, El thought, I will miss them. She frowned as she exited the restaurant.

Chapter 15

Gregor called El the next morning, and she went into a conference room so she could talk to him. "El, I have super news, I spoke to the hiring manager and she's really very interested in having you join the team. She agreed to increase the starting salary." He mentioned a figure that was a little higher and El was torn between being excited that asking had actually worked and being a little disappointed that it wasn't more. He talked about how she would be up for a salary review in six months and reminded her of the other benefits.

"Thank you. That's wonderful. I really appreciate that you checked with her and the offer was increased. It does sound like a great team and opportunity. I'd like to take a little time to think about it."

Gregor sounded disappointed that she hadn't immediately accepted but said that would be okay. He asked how soon she could get back to him. He wanted to know in 24 hours and she said she needed until the end of the next day. She wasn't sure if she wanted to push for any more time. After all, she should be able to make the decision by then, she thought.

After she hung up, she sat in the conference room for a few minutes and thought about how she felt. She wasn't as enthusiastic as she had hoped she'd be. She thought about what Teresa had said to her. She wondered if she was running away from her current job because she was annoyed or if this really was a good opportunity. She wasn't sure.

She texted Isabel a quick thank you and let her know that her advice had worked and she had gotten a higher offer. She let Teresa and Leticia know about her success also and they responded with happy emojis. The next message from Teresa read, "Are you going to take it?"

"Not sure," she replied.

"Okay, let me know if you want to talk," texted Teresa.

El thought about the job offer throughout the day. She thought about the pros and cons of leaving and still couldn't decide. That night El decided to talk to Mr. Fluffy. He could be a great listener if he wasn't busy sleeping. Unfortunately, he wasn't very good at giving advice.

She texted Jack and asked if he could talk. When he called her, she said she had a problem about which she needed some advice.

"This isn't some girl problem, is it, Rella?" he joked. "I'll give it a try but you know I'm not so good about that."

"Noooo, I wouldn't call you for that. I need to make a decision and I'm having a hard time. I thought you might be able to help me. I need a different perspective. That company I interviewed with offered me a higher salary…"

"Awesome! You made it happen," he said.

"Yes, but I don't know if I want it or not."

"Hmmm, okay. Describe the new job to me."

She told him about the company and the people she'd work for and the new industry.

"Okay," he said. "Now tell me about the job you'd be leaving."

She talked about her new projects and the presentation to the executives and lunch with Carl and Tom.

He interrupted her. "Rella, you already know."

"What are you talking about?"

"Go with the one you're more excited about. It's obvious when you talk about them that you like one more than another…"

"But…"

"No buts, listen to your bigger little brother. Even though you're pissed off at Tom, and you should be, you're obviously more interested in that one."

"But what if that's just nerves about the new job?"

"Remember the Clue game?"

El started laughing. It had been an ongoing joke with them after one birthday when she had gotten several games and dolls but all she talked about was the board game, Clue. She loved it and made him play it with her over and over. And they used to argue whether Colonel Mustard was better than Professor Plum and which one would be smarter.

He continued, "When you really like something you talk about it in a certain way. I'm not hearing that when you talk about the new job. You're not as enthusiastic as you were about Professor Plum."

She paused. "Thanks, I needed to hear that."

"That's what I'm here for."

They talked a few more minutes, and Jack asked her how she was doing overall. He made her promise to call if she needed anything.

The next morning El called Gregor at Proponics and thanked him for the opportunity and said she had decided not to take the job. She said she really appreciated the opportunity, but it wasn't the right move for her at that time. When she got off the phone, she felt that it had been the right thing to do. Interviewing for that job had made her realize what she liked about her current company. Yes, she was annoyed now but there were lots of possibilities. She decided to set up another meeting with PJ to talk about how she could start working on Tom to get her raise.

When she got back to her desk, she was surprised to see another meeting invitation with Kate for right before lunch. She quickly accepted and gathered some more information about the project in preparation for what the executive might want to ask her.

Kate's assistant told El to go right in. Kate was already sitting on the couch and gestured for El to join her. Today, she was dressed in a striped yellow and navy dress that exuded casual elegance. She thanked El for joining her.

"I'm happy to," said El. "I brought some new project information to review with you."

Kate waved her hand dismissively, and her heavy bracelets jangled. "I don't want to talk about the project. I want to talk about you."

"Me?" repeated El.

"Yes, I've heard great things about not only your project management skills but also your customer skills and insights. Where do you see yourself in the company?"

El's brain was trying to process this and her immediate thought was, don't sound like an idiot.

She smiled and used her favorite stalling technique, "Can you tell me more about that? What do you mean?" In her head, she was saying to herself, what would PJ do right now?

"What do you like to do, El? What's your interest? What do you want to do next?"

"I've been really excited to work on some of the new projects like the U.K. one and Intermedstar." She tried to channel PJ. "They've given me a chance to really make a difference with the customers and add to the bottom line. I want to do more of that, work with more groups and help them to leverage and build business."

"Good, good. I'm glad to hear that. I wanted to talk to you about a new opportunity. You may have heard that we're going to be making some changes with the new acquisition and product lines and we've decided to start a new group that will be responsible for developing innovative strategies. Imagine the Intermedstar project but on steroids. Based on the work you've done, it could be a good group for you."

El realized that this had suddenly turned from a meeting into an interview. She was glad she had recently had experience interviewing at Proponics, but she wished she had known about this in advance. She had only been reminded about the changes at lunch with Tom and Carl and she didn't know much about Kate or her area.

"That sounds really interesting. What would the group do exactly?"

"We would just start off with two managers and four specialists, but I see this as growing rather rapidly. The managers would report to a new Director of Strategy." She went on to describe more about the team's responsibilities and how she saw the team fitting into the company.

"Who would be the managers?" asked El, wondering who she might be reporting to.

"It hasn't been announced yet, so I expect that we can keep this between us. Carl Ryland will be one of the managers."

El tried to process that. At lunch the other day, she had wondered if Carl was looking to get Tom's job if Tom got promoted. She didn't expect that Carl would be moving to a totally different group.

Kate continued, "And you would be the other one."

El tried not to look surprised and just nodded. Getting a promotion to management wasn't easy. She was thinking that normally this is where she would say that she'd never directly managed anyone and she wasn't sure she could do it. And by the way, she wasn't sure she was the best person to work on strategy. She remembered that PJ had once said that men take jobs when they think they can do some of it and believe they can figure out the rest, but women don't want to take jobs unless they believe they can do almost all of it already. She forced herself to stay silent and not discount her abilities and talk Kate out of promoting her.

"Actually, Carl was the one who suggested that I talk to you. He was very impressed with what you did for him and his group. He thought you'd be a great addition the team. And after I saw you give that presentation, I agreed with him."

"Yes, I was really happy with what we were able to do. Carl is great to work with. We just had lunch the other day."

Kate smiled. "Good. Good." She described more about the job. El nodded and asked questions.

Kate said, "Of course, this is all an initial conversation. HR is already aware of this, but I wanted to chat with you first to see before we move any further. Is this something that might interest you?"

"Yes, it sounds like a great opportunity." She paused. "But what about Tom?"

Kate smiled. "Tom knows I'm talking to you. I talked to him first. He said he'd be sorry to have you leave his team, but he understood that this makes sense for the company and you."

They spoke a few more minutes about the job and Kate explained the next steps starting with filling out an internal application for the position.

El left the meeting and was happy it was lunch time. She got out of the building and walked down the street away from her usual lunch places. What she really wanted to do was to run down the street singing and dancing but she knew that'd look ridiculous. So instead, she ducked into a small Thai restaurant and ordered *pad kee mao* with chicken and a Thai coconut milk iced tea. Then she texted PJ immediately to let her know what was going on. She also texted Leticia and Teresa, though she would rather FaceTime them. But she didn't want to chance anyone from her company overhearing her screaming with joy at the possibility of moving into management very soon. Leticia sent back an immediate text saying they were meeting her at the cantina at 5:30 to celebrate and that she was buying.

El responded, "Awesome. Thank you."

She texted with the three women and her brother while she ate her noodles, and then she left with a few minutes to spare on her lunchtime break. She used those minutes to stop by a nearby bakery and buy a big chocolate chip cookie.

When El returned to the office, she marched straight to Carl's space and set the cookie on his desk, to the left of where he sat typing. "I owe you a big thank you," El said. "I was summoned to Kate's office this morning."

He stared at the cookie. "Ah, what a fun surprise. Thanks. I was happy to do that."

"You didn't order dessert the other day at lunch but sounded like you wanted some so I thought I'd get you a treat," El said. "I really appreciate that you recommended me to Kate. Thank you. I'm excited about using my skills in a new position and working closely with you."

"We work well together, El." Carl rattled off what he knew about Kate, including how she liked to work with her managers and some personal details about her. She loved pugs and had two named Montague and Capulet, who were pretty much her children. She had hiked both the Pacific Coast and the Appalachian Trails. And rumor was she was the best golfer in the company, and she had played at the collegiate level on Stanford's team.

In previous years, El would have thought Carl was frivolously gossiping, but now she knew that he was providing her with valuable information that could help her connect with the person who most likely would become her new boss. "Thank you for telling me all of that, Carl. You're a wonderful colleague and friend."

Carl reminded her that though listing references on the internal application was optional, he'd be happy to be one for her, and he was sure Tom would be, too. He told her to fill out the application as soon as possible as they were planning on naming the managers soon and setting up the team. "It's moving a lot faster than the way some things here happen, but without the team in place, they really can't grow that business line or capitalize on the investment."

El said she understood and would get it done as soon as she got back to her desk. She thanked Carl again and then went to her own cubicle to do just that.

At 5:15 she left the office so she wouldn't be late getting to the cantina. Leticia sat facing the door on a stool at a high table. She was wearing a streamlined black power suit and a royal blue silk tank top. The red soles of her high heels were the only other color in her outfit as she had forgone any jewelry that day. Teresa had her back to the door, but El could see she was dressed in her usual fashion, which they had nicknamed "hippie chic". She had paired a flowy floral short dress over black leggings, which were tucked into short black boots. Her hair was loose and hung long, which was rare for her. El admired them from the doorway, for their beauty and distinctive style, and for their years of friendship and support.

When Leticia saw her she shouted, "There's our rock star now." She hugged El and said, "Look at you go. See what happens when we listen to our inner voices and our friends. We get even better than our initial offers." She laughed.

Teresa and El hugged and Teresa signaled the bartender for a drink for El.

"Absolutely," said El. "And Jack. I listened to him, too. Who would have thunk I'd be asking my little brother for career advice." She smiled. "But as squirrelly as he's been sometimes, he's always known how to listen to his intuition and been unafraid to follow it. He helped me listen to mine by pointing out where my passions lie."

The bartender put a margarita on the rocks with no salt in front of El, and the women all raised their glasses. El said, "To friends who hold the ladder as you climb."

"Here, here," Teresa and Leticia said in unison. And then Teresa said to Leticia, "Are you buying food for us, too?" which made El and Leticia laugh.

"Of course. A celebration isn't complete without canapés. Isn't the app in happy hour referencing appetizers?" She smiled.

"It must," Teresa said, as she motioned the bartender again and ordered chips, salsa, and guacamole; *sopes surtidos*; and a vegetarian version of ceviche.

El filled them in on the call with Gregor, the meeting she had with Kate, the cookie she bought Carl, and the internal application that she spent a portion of the afternoon filling out. Teresa asked the timeline for the hiring process and what the next steps were. Leticia asked if she had any idea how much more money she might be paid. El answered the questions as best she could but realized she didn't know, especially the salary question. She made a note in her phone to find out the timeline of the process from Kate (and to send Kate a thank you e-mail for the meeting).

As the food arrived at the table and after they ordered a second round of drinks, Teresa told them about the class she had started taking so she could advance herself in her company. She enthused about the teacher and how much she had learned in the first two weeks.

When the drinks came, they raised their glasses and congratulated Teresa. She thanked them and then paused and looked down. "But there's something I'm wondering," she said and paused again.

"Out with it, girl" said Leticia, laughing.

"Well, El has done such a great job asking for a raise and negotiating with that other company. I just wonder if maybe I should think about asking for a raise, too." She shook her head. "But that's probably not a good idea. I mean the company just started spending money on me for this training. That might seem too pushy."

El thought about what she'd learned from PJ, Isabel, and Shayla. "Don't stop yourself! It already sounds like you're talking yourself out of it. And by the way, there are probably two different buckets of money, one for training and one for raises."

"Exactly," said Leticia. "Go for it. What do you have to lose?"

"Easy for you," said Teresa. "But I don't want to get my new boss mad. I don't want her to think I'm ungrateful."

"She's shown that she does value what you're doing and how it can help her and the team. Asking for a raise can show her that you recognize your value. Believe me, I know it's scary! But I think it's one of those things that gets easier when you keep doing it. You won't know though unless you start. Let's talk it through. When was the last time you got a raise?" El asked.

"Last year. But it was really small. Actually, all my raises have been really small. The boss always said that they wanted to give more, I was doing a great job, but money's tight, blah, blah, blah."

They talked more about the situation and El said, "What would a successful guy do?"

Teresa laughed and said that he'd ask for it and wouldn't feel bad about it. "But I don't know what to say."

"How about something like, I'm really excited about this new group and I want to make sure I'm on the right track. I'd like to talk to you about what I need to do to get a larger raise in the future," said El.

"Yes, and tell them they can stick their tiny little raises…" started Leticia.

El interrupted, "No. Say, my last raises were small even though my manager said I was doing a great job and wanted to give me more. I want to find out from you what your expectations are."

Teresa pointed at Leticia, "Not gonna do that." And they all laughed. She practiced saying El's recommended words a few times and her friends coached her.

"What do you think?" asked El.

Teresa nodded. "I think I can do it." Her friends cheered and she promised to give them an update.

Before the evening ended, El asked for dating updates. She had wondered if her friends didn't volunteer the information because they were being sensitive about her breakup with Derek. Leticia admitted that Jackson had been calling her to go out again, but she had been putting him off. While her 30-hour date with him had been a blast, she wasn't sure she wanted to see where it went. "I'm so busy with work that I'm not sure I have time for someone," she said.

El said, "Don't you think if you were really feeling it, you would make the time?"

"Maybe," Leticia conceded. "But right now I feel like my life is full."

"To full lives and making time for friends," Teresa raised her glass and they toasted.

"So what about you, T? How's Mr. Dancing Shoes?" El asked.

Teresa grinned. "He's fabulous. I'm seeing him again this weekend and we talk or text every day." Teresa's eyes were bright.

"Oh no," Leticia joked, "she's been bitten by the love bug. Just look at that dreamy look in her eyes. You're toast, girlfriend."

Teresa was suddenly serious. "I may be. I've never met anyone like him, and I've never felt so connected to anyone before."

"Good for you," El said. "Good for you. When do we get to meet him?"

"Yes, when do we vet this choice of yours?" Leticia wiggled her eyebrows, which made El and Teresa crack up.

"You're too much," Teresa said. "Maybe we can go to that new wine bar on Sunday afternoon and you can meet us there. I'll text you."

"Sunday works for me," Leticia said.

"Me too," said El.

The evening ended with hugs and El thought again how lucky she was to have such dear friends.

The next day she was interviewed by a recruiter in HR, Phil, whom she had known from a training class they had taken together the previous year. They chatted a bit and he told her more about the job duties and title. He mentioned that the new director in charge of the group, Rachel, had been hired and would start on Monday. El could talk to her then and a final decision would be made at that time.

She messaged PJ with an update and asked for any suggestions. Her message back was brief, "You've got this! I know you can do it. Go for it!" El smiled and thought, yes, I am ready.

Over the weekend, El researched the new director online to find out more about her. She learned that Rachel and Kate had worked at the same company several years ago and wondered if she had known her then. El listened to her play list starting with "Try Everything" by Shakira, a favorite from "Zootopia". She sang the lyrics as she updated the interview notes she had developed for Proponics and included examples of how she had indirectly supervised people on projects.

On Monday morning, she met with Rachel in her new office. Rachel was very friendly and complimented El on her success with the recent projects. El had been expecting more of an interview, but instead the new director talked more about her expectations and how she thought El could fit into those plans.

A little later that morning, El was called to meet with Phil, the recruiter, again. He said that Rachel had agreed that she was the right person for the job and they wanted to offer her the position. He told her that she would be moved to a management grade level and told her what her new salary would be. El paused. It was a good increase. She wondered if she should just be happy with it and accept it. Then she thought back to what she had learned from Isabel and what she had told Teresa. What did she have to lose?

She smiled and talked about how excited she was about the job and what a great fit it was. Then she said, "Is there any flexibility with the salary?"

Phil said, "What do you mean? This is a substantial increase from where you are now."

"Yes, and I do appreciate it. I'm very excited about the job. I also know that this is a big change in responsibility, visibility, and connection to the bottom line." El forced herself to stop. She felt bad putting Phil in a difficult situation, but she remembered that Isabel had told her this was the time when you had the most leverage.

"This is a new position so I don't think so, but I'll be happy to check for you." Phil said.

El thanked him and again told him how excited she was about the opportunity and what a good fit it was.

She had a hard time focusing on her work for the next few hours. She kept wondering if she had made a mistake. Sure, she had followed PJ's advice, but maybe she shouldn't have asked for more money this time. The more she thought about it, the more she really wanted this new job. She hoped she hadn't messed it up. Especially with a new director. This was Rachel's first day. What was she going to think about her?

By the time she got a message from Phil asking for a quick phone call, she had convinced herself that she should not have asked for the additional money. She went into a conference room, took a deep breath, called Phil, and prepared for the worst.

"Hi, El, I have good news for you. They agreed to a higher salary." He mentioned an increase. It wasn't an enormous change, only a couple of thousand dollars, but it was an increase.

"Thank you. That is so great to hear. I really appreciate you checking for me."

Phil chuckled. "Frankly, I think Rachel liked the fact that you asked. You're going to have to negotiate with different teams in the new job and that showed off your willingness to ask for what you want."

El laughed. She was so relieved. "Thanks. I definitely want the job. What do I need to do to get started?"

"You just did it. I'll let them know that you accepted and generate the paperwork. This will be effective in a few days, and we'd appreciate it if you would not mention anything about this yet until you get the signed paperwork and we're ready to announce it."

"What about Tom?"

"Don't worry. I'll let him know. He's already expecting this."

El thanked Phil and took a deep breath when she hung up the phone. She texted her friends and said the celebration would be on her as soon as she got the signed paperwork. This was going to be a great week. She focused on getting her current job done and started thinking about her new role.

Rachel's arrival had been announced earlier in the day, but there was no mention of the new department that she'd be heading. El assumed that would be coming soon.

First thing on Thursday morning all employees in the office were called into the main room. Marc announced some changes. He would be taking a new role in a different office and Tom would be taking over his position, but there would be some adjustments. The group that El was a part of was being disbanded in order to serve the corporate direction better. Most of the people would be moved to different groups; however, there would be a few reductions in force and those people were meeting with HR representatives during this meeting.

El looked around and realized some of the people she worked with on a regular basis were not in the room. She got a sick feeling in her stomach. She realized that her move to the other group was all part of a major corporate reorg. She was glad she was in the room and would be kept on, but she wondered where she would be if she hadn't taken the new job.

She half listened to Marc thanking those people for their service and stating his belief that this was going to be a positive move for the company and its customers. Carl was across the room and caught her eye and winked. El smiled at him. She was thrilled they were going to the same place and would navigate a new group and boss together.

When El returned to her desk, she suddenly remembered Ann and how she had helped El on this journey. She texted, "You available for drinks?"

"Always. You buying?"

"Absolutely. I'll tell you what we're celebrating when I see you f2f. 5:15 @ Martini Bar?"

"CU."

El had a hard time concentrating on work that day. The office seemed unnaturally quiet. Her thoughts kept going back to her former co-workers who had been walked out earlier. She tried to stay out of the gossip as people quietly shared what they had heard. She thought back to a previous company when she had lost her job. She knew that these decisions were good for the companies, but it was hard to think that it's business not personal when it affected you.

She was glad to escape the office and head to the Martini Bar. She got a table and ordered a drink along with some chicken skewers and house-made potato chips. As she waited for Ann, she thought about all the things that had changed since they had talked. She shook her head in wonder, and then she remembered she should probably text Leticia and Teresa about the layoff and assure them she was okay.

When she looked up from her phone, El saw Ann's spiky blue hair through the crowd. Her friend was dressed all in black today and, as usual, looked more like a goth art student than a corporate manager. After she approached the table, Ann gave El a quick hug and sat down. "What's new?"

El laughed and said, "Everything!"

Ann looked surprised. "Okay, I'm intrigued. Tell me more."

El started by thanking her friend for her advice when they had gotten together last time. She told her how things had worked out with Tom and the desk problem. El paused and realized that seemed so far in the past.

Ann congratulated her and El quickly said, "But wait, there's more." She talked about asking Tom for a raise, getting turned down, meeting with Proponics, and Kate's job offer. Ann shook her head and El put up her hand and said, "And then there was today…"

Ann started to laugh and said, "Are you kidding?"

"Nope," said El and quickly mentioned the corporate restructure and lay-offs.

Ann sat back, surprised. "Wow."

The waitress stopped by the table. Ann said, "I definitely need a drink," and ordered a local craft beer. "Anything else?"

"Oh yeah. Derek and I broke up because he decided to move to Asia for a while and acted like a jerk."

"Are you okay?"

"Yeah, I'm okay. It wasn't fun, but it's the right thing."

Ann smiled. "Good for you. I think that was probably a smart choice for you."

El looked at her friend. "Oh yeah?"

"Just looking at the facts," she said. "He was always more focused on himself, in my humble opinion."

El took a sip. "True, so true."

Ann asked questions about the changes. When her drink came, she raised her glass and said, "To you, for taking charge and making it happen."

"But I couldn't have done it without you." El thanked Ann for helping her to focus on the facts and to not get upset at work. She went on to tell Ann about how others had also helped her. Ann asked about what she had learned from PJ and Shayla and Isabel, and El shared her insights.

They ended the night promising to get together again soon. El was again reminded how lucky she was to have such great friends.

When El checked her e-mail that night, she found a LinkedIn message from a headhunter who had heard about the company's downsizing. El was about to ignore it and then decided that it wouldn't hurt to connect. Even if she didn't want a job now, maybe she could recommend someone. After all, she was happy with her new role, but she had learned that things could quickly change in the future.

The next morning, El worked to wrap up some of her projects so she could move to her new role. News of her promotion had gotten out and people congratulated her. As El talked to her co-workers, she thought about how just a few months earlier she would have been looking at someone who moved to a new role with envy, wondering how she had made it happen. She was thankful for that first meeting on the plane with

PJ that started this journey.

When she had a moment free, she sent a message to PJ asking to set up another meeting. El had already texted her about the promotion but she wanted to take her out to thank her for all her help. PJ said that would have to wait as she was traveling on business, but they scheduled time for a video conference the next day. That night, El spent some time jotting down notes.

Right before she was going to meet with PJ, El saw an e-mail from Isabel. She was surprised to read that Isabel wanted her to speak to a women's group she belonged to. El grimaced. Speaking in front of groups made her nervous but she had promised PJ that she would share what she had learned. She knew PJ would be happy to hear about it.

El smiled when she saw PJ's familiar face appear on the screen, her dark curls pulled tightly back, in a way El had never seen before. Before El could say anything, PJ clapped enthusiastically, "Congratulations! You kicked ass! Good for you!"

El laughed and said, "PJ, it's all because of you!"

PJ snorted. "That's a load of crap. YOU did it."

"But, you gave me the ideas…"

"Yes, and you did something with it," she interrupted.

"I really want to thank you. I can't say enough, what meeting you meant to me." PJ started to interrupt and El held up her hand. "Please, you've been a lifesaver. You helped me to think about things differently and to have the confidence to act on them. Thank you."

PJ smiled broadly and said, "You're welcome. I want to thank you for giving me the opportunity to talk with you. I was impressed by your willingness to look at what you were doing and to try new things. I'm so happy to hear what's going on."

El told her about the new job, new manager, company reorganization, and layoffs. They talked about the changes. Then El said, "I want to let you know how much I appreciated going through the PJ Master's Degree Program with you. I put together a list of what I've learned.

PJ laughed and nodded, "Sounds great. Tell me."

El held up a piece of paper, "Let me show it to you." She had created a page with a colorful list. She read, "What I Learned About Business:

#1 It's business, it's not personal (even when it feels personal). Keep negative emotions out of it.

#2 Look and sound confident, even when I may not feel confident.

#3 Work with my boss and understand what's important to him or her.

#4 Ask for what I want. Then stop talking. Don't say, I'm sorry.

#5 Respond positively no matter what the answer is. "No" answers can change.

#6 Ask myself what would a successful guy do?

#7 Focus on me and what's right for me. My company doesn't love me. My family and friends do.

#8 Keep learning from others."

El paused and waved the paper at her. "Thank you so much. This has meant a lot to me."

PJ was smiling. "I love it! Will you send me a copy?"

"It's on its way."

"And besides helping your friend Teresa, how are you going to pay all of this fabulous information forward and help other women?"

El told PJ about Isabel's invitation. "It won't be a large group, maybe a dozen women, but it's a start," El said. "And I will continue to look for opportunities to connect with other women. I've found a few private Facebook groups, and I've asked to join. Some are industry-focused but others have been created so women in business can support their sisters."

"Good for you," PJ said. "The information is too powerful to keep from sharing it. It's a way for women to advance themselves and gain equity."

El's eyes sparkled and she joked, "It's our version of bibbidi-bobbidi-boo."

PJ laughed. "You've certainly transformed."

"And I even kicked the prince to the curb when he turned into a toad." El laughed at the irony and the mixing of fairy tale metaphors. "Thank you, fairy godmother full of Patience."

PJ laughed. "You had to throw that in there, huh?"

El grinned. "Bring Shayla and let's celebrate my journey when you return. Dinner on me and my new salary." She kissed her fingers and blew PJ a kiss. "Text me."

Chapter 16

Two months later, El was taking deep breaths in her car getting ready to speak to the local Women in Business group. She had already spent two minutes in her Amy Cuddy Power Pose to get ready. As she took another cleansing breath, she reminded herself that she had willingly accepted this invitation to speak. She wanted to share what she had learned. *Yes*, she said to herself, *but that's when I thought it would be just a dozen women in a room chatting.* It turned out that the "little event" that Isabel had invited her to had changed to a group of almost 50.

Isabel was on the board of the group and had explained that they were a mixed industry group of women who supported other women's success. When Isabel had proposed the idea to the rest of the board, they enthusiastically agreed and invited two other speakers for a panel.

El nervously looked at the invitation on her phone that said, "A Look Back and A Look Forward—What I Wish I Had Known. Three leaders share their insights to help you succeed."

She had met the other two speakers by phone in preparation for this meeting and was in awe about what they had accomplished. The noisy little voice in the back of her head told her that she didn't deserve to be with the other speakers; why did she think people would want to listen to her? She took another breath and told the voice to hush. She briefly closed her eyes and imagined a positive mind movie where she looked calm and the audience was happy and clapped loudly at the end.

She opened her eyes, walked into the building, and found the small meeting room where she waited for the other speakers. She resisted the urge to look down and check her phone and instead kept her body language open and confident while she focused on what she would say.

When the other speakers arrived, they chatted and compared notes. At the start of the meeting, they walked to the front of the room and sat down. Isabel welcomed everyone and had each of the speakers introduce themselves. Then she started asking the questions that she had sent them in advance.

When it was El's turn to talk about her success journey, she shared the story about meeting PJ on the plane and learning from her and others. She briefly told about asking for a raise, getting turned down, and then getting the promotion. She wrapped it up with her suggestions. "I've learned three key things. First, be in a continual state of learning. Find resources and people you can learn from. And they may be in unexpected places. My brother, who runs a food truck, gave me some great advice.

"Second, you have to ask. Whether it's a raise or a promotion, a new job opportunity or something in your personal life, you need to ask for what you want. Don't expect other people to read your mind and just give you what you want. If you don't ask, you don't get.

"Third, you need to stop stopping yourself. Many women, like me, have spent a lot of time apologizing and limiting themselves. Have big dreams and make them happen. Don't wait. I heard a great quote recently, 'The waves don't stop, take the boat and go.' There will never be a perfect time to do something, don't wait.

"Oh and one other thing, make sure to help other women. We need to support each other."

El felt a rush of excitement when she had finished. She had presented it clearly and confidently and felt that she got the message out. She knew PJ would be proud. She had sent a text of encouragement earlier that day.

Isabel opened it up for questions. El had been dreading this part because she couldn't prepare for it, but she was ready.

One participant asked how they dealt with nervousness. One of the other speakers, a senior leader who had recently been promoted to Vice President, talked about how she felt the fear and kept going. El mentioned Shayla's suggestion about using positive mind movies to help shift her focus away from things she was worried about.

Another participant asked how they handled dealing with their managers. "Weren't you worried that your boss would be mad at you?" El smiled to herself as she considered how she had thought the same thing just a few months previously. She shared PJ's comments that successful men don't worry about that because they understand that it's part of business. "Actually, when I got this job offer, I asked for more money and I was concerned that my new boss would react badly but it turned out that she was impressed that I wanted to negotiate. It let her see my skills. Don't be afraid to negotiate with your manager as long as it's professional and positive. I know it worked for me."

After a few more questions, the meeting ended. Isabel thanked the panelists and they chatted for a few minutes before moving to the coffee and snacks in the back of the room.

El felt so relieved. Her shoulders relaxed. She hadn't realized how tense she had been. Even though she had prepared, speaking in front of a group didn't come naturally to her.

Several women stopped her and thanked her for her suggestions. One woman said, "It meant so much to me to hear that you didn't let it stop you when you didn't get a raise. I've been afraid to ask because I was so worried about what would happen if they said no. You've helped me to realize that it's okay. It's all right to hear no. I'm going to work on this and ask for a raise this week. Thank you!"

El said, "Good for you! I'm so glad you found what I said helpful." She pulled a card out of her bag and handed it to the woman. "Why don't you let me know how it goes." The other woman's eyes got big and she smiled broadly as she took the card and handed El one of hers. "Thank you. Yes, I'll do that."

Another woman introduced herself to El. "Hi, I'm Cathi. I loved your presentation. It made so much sense and gave me such great ideas. I wonder, you said that you should ask for what you want. And you said that we should learn from others." She paused briefly. "Do you think I could contact you and ask you some follow up questions? I'd love to learn from you."

El smiled and thought about when she had asked PJ to help her and how much had changed since then. She remembered that PJ only asked her in return to take action and share what she learned with others.

"Sure," she said. "Thanks for asking. Here's my card. Why don't you send me a message and we can set up a time." Cathi smiled, handed El her business card, and promised that she would.

After all, if you don't ask, you don't get.

The End

Authors' Notes

While El, PJ, and their colleagues, friends, and family members are all fictitious, the scenarios in this book are not; they are based on both of our careers and experiences and that of our friends' and co-workers'.

We dedicate this book to our daughters, Julianne Browne and Shannon Heckt, because they inspire us, move us, and make us laugh, and because like El, they are figuring out how to navigate their 20s, their professional and personal relationships, and their careers.

Laura would like to thank some amazing women who have inspired and supported her career: Amy Gonzales (Vice President Global Learning and Development, WOMEN Unlimited), Barbara Limmer (Career Coach and Consultant), Jill Clark (Business Coach and Leadership Champion), Patty Cardellino (OD and Leadership Expert) and Sherri Thomas (President, CareerCoaching360.com).

About the Authors

This is the second collaborative book between Laura C. Browne and Jill L. Ferguson. The first was *Raise Rules for Women: How To Make More Money At Work* (In Your Face Ink, 2008).

Laura C. Browne is the voice of Careertipsforwomen.com, a business coach who has worked with hundreds of women in all stages of their careers, a corporate trainer, and the author of eight books. She can be reached at laura.browne@careertipsforwomen.com.

Jill L. Ferguson is an artist, business and higher education consultant, a book and entrepreneur coach, and the founder of Women's Wellness Weekends and Creating the Freelance Career, plus she is an award-winning writer and author of nine books. She can be reached at jill@jillferguson.com.

www.ingramcontent.com/pod-product-compliance
Lightning Source LLC
LaVergne TN
LVHW041155080426
835511LV00006B/606

9 780692 041536